DR. ADAM CLARKE

Methodist Preacher and Scholar

Herbert Boyd McGonigle

MA, BD, DD, PHD

Former Lecturer at Nazarene Theological College, Dene Road, Didsbury, Manchester, in the classes in Church History, Theology and Wesley Studies, Former Principal of Nazarene Theological College and now Principal Emeritus

British Library Cataloguing in Publication Data.
A catalogue record for this book is available from the British Library

ISBN 978 0 86071 699 0

A Commissioned Publication of

tel: 0115 932 0643 web: www.moorleys.co.uk

FOREWORD

I am delighted that Bill Graham has offered to write the Foreword. When Jeanne and I moved to Manchester, we came to know Bill and Lorraine about thirty-eight years ago and we are still friends today! When the Wesley Fellowship was begun they quickly joined it and for almost thirty years, Bill was editor of The Wesley Fellowship Bulletin *and I was Chairman. He published the following books;* Wesley's Early Experiments in Education: With Special Reference to Girls at Kingwood School *(1990);* Pupils in the Gospel: The Education of John Wesley's Preachers *(2002); and,* 'Sent by My Lord, On You I Call': Reflections on the Genesis of John Wesley's Preaching *(2013). Across the years he has edited and published scores of the Wesley Fellowship services and has kept up his writing and his studies. Bill is a graduate of the Open University, Manchester Metropolitan University (CNAA), the University of Manchester, with graduate and postgraduate qualifications in Science, Education, Psychology and Management; after around forty years of service as a Primary School teacher, he is now retired and a Life Member of the National Association of Head Teachers. Bill and Lorraine have kept up friendships with Jeanne and me and he is just the person to write on Adam Clarke! Be sure that you read his encouragement in the Foreword and all the help given to me across thirty years to the end of my appreciation.*

It was in 1988 that the Revd. Dr. Herbert Boyd McGonigle, the author of this very welcome and most interesting little volume, first told me he had an ambition 'to one day write of the life of Adam Clarke.' I am certain of the year, because we were travelling by car, with Herbert's wife, Jeanne, to Morley, Yorkshire, where Herbert would be speaking at a church meeting arranged to celebrate the 250th anniversary of the conversion of John and Charles Wesley in May 1738. We can be sure that it is not due to a lack of the biographer's personal enthusiasm for his subject! It was clear to me even all those years ago that Herbert had a special affinity for Dr. Adam Clarke. After all, the two men had been born and bred (albeit about 180 years apart) in Ulster, the most northerly province of Ireland – and this land, and its people, held for each man a lasting place in their hearts, despite each spending most of their years as exiles serving their Lord in other parts of the British

Isles. Indeed it would seem that Herbert's given name of 'Boyd' is common to both men's ancestry, and suggesting a genealogical family heritage pointing back to the 'plantation' in Ulster of Protestant people from Great Britain promoted by King James I in the seventeenth-century. Significantly, it was in the Emerald Isle that both men had been saved, and their lives transformed, when, as teenagers, they first responded to the gospel of Jesus Christ, their Saviour and Lord. Furthermore, both these Irishmen had been deeply influenced by the life and teaching of John and Charles Wesley.

Although experiences in Herbert's life prior to 1988 can hardly be considered as direct reasons for the delay in his beginning to write a biography of Adam Clarke, they may help to explain the context that led to his decision to do so. In the spring of 1988, Dr. McGonigle had been in post for less than two years as Principal of the institution then known as British Isles Nazarene College (BINC). He could look back over the previous twenty-eight busy years to 1960 when he was awarded a diploma from Hurlet Nazarene College in Manchester. It recorded passes 'with distinction' in a long list of subjects, including Homiletics, Church History, Biblical Exegesis and Systematic Theology, all demonstrating Herbert's remarkable ability for learning and scholarship – not unlike the gifted ability possessed by Adam Clarke (although, when they were boys, both men had received only fairly basic formal educational experiences in Ireland). Following Bible college, Herbert had gone on to serve as a much loved pastor at churches in England and Scotland, as well as becoming internationally recognised as a gifted preacher, and writer of numerous articles (occasionally referring to Adam Clarke) in periodicals such as the *Flame*, *The Preacher Magazine*, the *Herald of Holiness* and the *Wesleyan Theological Journal*. This Christian service, coupled with success following studies for degrees from the universities of London (BD, 1975) and Leeds (MA, 1976), had led to his appointment in September 1976 as a full-time lecturer at BINC. This was a record of multi-tasking not unlike that of Adam Clarke – who was a popular Methodist itinerant preacher, who published much, and also found himself being awarded the degrees of MA (1806) and LLD (1808) from King's College, University of Aberdeen. Moreover, for a short period around 1983, Herbert had even found himself elected (into a role he did not seek) as Superintendent Minister for the Church of the Nazarene British Isles South District – a position of denominational leadership similar to, but perhaps not quite on the same scale as that of Adam Clarke, who was (sometimes reluctantly) elected three times President of the British Methodist Conference (1806, 1814, and 1822), and also President of the Irish Methodist Conference on no less than four occasions (1811, 1812, 1816, and 1822).

However, it is only from 1988 that we can see clearly the *particular* reasons why Dr. McGonigle decided to postpone his personal desire to write a biography of Clarke – *it was to deal with the more urgent, indeed pivotal needs of the college.* As Principal, he had realised that if the college was to prosper and keep up with rapidly changing international trends in higher education, more members of the faculty (himself included) would need to undertake further research in order to add a PhD degree to their academic credentials. Although Herbert had co-founded and chaired The Wesley Fellowship from 1985, and over the years had already become widely recognised (just like Adam Clarke in his time) as a notable authority on the Wesley family, not even the impressive award of an honorary degree of Doctor of Divinity by Olivet Nazarene University in 1992 would suffice for Herbert. Demands on him as Principal had already led to the time placed on him to complete a PhD at Leeds expiring - causing him to pause, and later begin on a new PhD with Keele University, eventually receiving the Keele doctorate in 1994, with his 'valuable and deeply researched' thesis and being published as *Sufficient Saving Grace: John Wesley's Evangelical Arminianism,* in 2001.

In the summer of 2004, Dr. McGonigle retired as Principal of NTC (Nazarene Theological College) but continued to give some time to his role as a Senior Research Fellow and Senior Lecturer in Church History and Wesley Studies. However, again putting aside any personal ambition to begin his biography of Dr. Clarke, Herbert devoted himself as Director of the Manchester Wesley Research Centre (MWRC), to capitalise on the opportunities provided by these new partnerships. Under his leadership both the number of research students enrolled with MWRC, and the number of new further partner institutions involved, had grown significantly. Now with his new title of Principal Emeritus, he has returned to writing. One of the fruits has been the production of this attractive and long awaited new book on Adam Clarke. Dr. McGonigle has honoured me with his invitation to write a foreword to his book. This has proved to be a blessing in that it has enabled me to enjoy reading not only what Herbert has written but also to benefit from reading carefully through the substantial quotations he has made from the writings of Adam Clarke. Herbert shows clearly in his text how some more recent 'holiness' writers have misunderstood Clarke by now themselves reading carefully what he wrote, rather than relying on brief misquotes by others. He has produced in retirement, with the background encouragement and support of Jeanne and their family, such informative, interesting and handy volumes on Wesleyan theology and history.

Herbert brings out in this book that Adam Clarke was an amazingly gifted and complex man, who, over the years has been described or thought of in a variety of different ways. Perhaps Herbert's own description, originally published in *The Preacher Magazine*, describing Adam Clarke as a 'holiness saint and scholar.... and as an ardent, convinced expositor of scriptural holiness…. whose name is synonymous with biblical scholarship' gives some indications of what he sets out to tell us in this book. And so, as I thank Herbert for introducing me to a closer acquaintance with the remarkable life and work of Dr. Adam Clarke, I commend this book to you the reader.

William T. Graham
May 28, 2015.

DR. ADAM CLARKE
Methodist Preacher and Scholar

When Dr. Adam Clarke is mentioned our thoughts need to go back two-and-a-half centuries, because he can be numbered amongst those people who knew such towering figures as John Wesley (1703-1791), John Fletcher (1729-1785), William Bramwell (1759-1816) and Samuel Bradburn (1751-1816). Clarke was born in 1760 and died of cholera in 1832. Today his commentary on the Bible is still well known, and he is remembered as a preacher, scholar and man of the Word. He was the greatest name in the Methodist generation which followed John Wesley. He had not the missionary zeal of Dr. Coke (1747-1814), he was not an orator of the class of Samuel Bradburn, nor did he have the theological acumen of Richard Watson (1781-1833), but in a combination of gifts and fire, he surpassed them all. Who was he - and what made him so famous?

The name Adam Clarke points us back in British history to the times of the later Hanoverian kings - George III, George IV and William IV; and it is now more than thirty years since a book on Clarke was published, and that was in America[1]; and it is over fifty years since a book on him was published in Europe, and that was in Ireland.[2] And yet the Clarke family was English in origin, having gone over to Ireland in the 17th century and settled in Antrim. William Clarke, the grandfather of Adam Clarke, married into the Boyd family. John Clarke, the eldest son of William, was intended for the Church of Ireland and he studied at Edinburgh and Glasgow. He entered Trinity College, Dublin, but a severe fever induced him to return home and a new occupation of teaching became his life. About 1758, John, with his wife and son, embarked on a ship with the intention of sailing for the British colonies in America where someone had suggested he might gain a professorship in one of the universities of the New World. His father arrived just as the ship was about to sail and

---

[1]   Wesley Tracy, *When Adam Clarke Preached People Listened* (Kansas City, Missouri: Beacon Hill Press, 1981); hereafter cited as 'Tracy'.

[2]   Robert Gallagher, *Adam Clarke: Saint and Scholar* (Belfast: Wesley Historical Society (Irish Branch), 1963); hereafter cited as 'Gallagher'.

prevailed upon his son to change their plans and return home with him.[3] John Clarke, with his family, eventually settled in the small village of Moybeg, in the parish of Kilcronaghan, in County Londonderry; and here his second son, Adam, was born in (or just after) 1760. John Clarke took up teaching and was a headmaster until his death. Their eldest son, Tracy, was given a classical education and when the time to decide on a profession came, he expressed a desire to study medicine. He went to Dublin and studied anatomy under Dr. Cleghorne. He applied to the Royal Navy as a surgeon, but when that proved impossible, he went as surgeon on a 'Guinea' ship. After two journeys, disgusted by his experience of the ship's slave trade, he returned to Magull, near Liverpool, married and had an extensive practice. He died there in 1802, leaving a wife, four sons and a daughter.

The Clarke's second child had been named Adam at the request of his paternal grand-parents, in memory of a son they had lost in early life. Adam was reared at first by his grand-parents, and as a young boy he was remarkably fit and healthy. He returned to his parents when he was

The house in Ulster, situated in Ballyaherton, Coleraine, Co. Londonderry

six-years-old and the family moved from Moybeg to Maghera, sixteen miles south of Coleraine. Two years later they moved to Garva, a village some ten miles distant, but still in Co. Londonderry. The family resided here till Adam was about twelve, and then they moved to the parish of Agherton in another part of the county, some miles

---

[3]   [Mary Ann Smith]. *An Account of the Infancy, Religious and Literary Life of Adam Clarke: written by one who was intimately acquainted with him from his boyhood to the sixtieth year of his age* (3 vols; ed. J. B. B. Clarke; London: T.S. Clarke, 1833), Vol. 1, p.15; hereafter cited as '*Account*'.

from Coleraine. The family had increased and the two boys now had five sisters. Their father, John Clarke, needed to keep a small farm in the limited time he had free from his teaching responsibilities. So, on alternate days, Adam was dispatched to look after the cattle and sheep. Adam was strong physically but his mental powers seemed to be developing more slowly. He found it difficult to even acquire the alphabet - and his father, who had set his heart on his son becoming a scholar, tried to awaken his intellect with harsh words and sterner discipline. When he was about six-years-old, a schoolmaster from a nearby school called into the school where Adam was a pupil. When Adam was called out and presented to the visitor, he was described as a 'grievous dunce', but the visiting master put a hand on the boy's head, and said: 'Never fear, Sir, this lad will make a good scholar yet.'[4] This was the first encouragement that young Adam had heard, and it helped him to think that he might prosper intellectually. Remembering this event long after, when he was nearing the age of seventy, Adam Clarke emphasized the importance of encouraging youngsters in their education.

> How injudicious is the general mode of dealing with those who are called *dull boys*. To every child learning must be a task, and as no young person is able to comprehend…. that the acquisition of learning will [be worth the effort involved], encouragement and kind words from the teacher are indispensably necessary to induce the learner to undergo the toil of these gymnastic exercises. *Wilful idleness* and neglect should be reprehended and punished, but where genius has not yet been unfolded, nor reason acquired its proper seat, the mildest methods [are the best]: and the smallest progress should be watched, and commended, that it may excite to farther attention and diligence. With those who are called *dull boys*, this method rarely fails. But there are very few teachers who possess the happy art of developing genius. They have not a sufficiency of penetration to find out the bent or characteristic propensity of the minds of their pupils, in order to give them the requisite excitement or direction.[5]

Adam Clarke's mother, a Presbyterian, was Scottish and she gave her time to the training up of all seven of her children. In later life Adam, speaking of his mother, said: 'I had a godly puritanic mother…. For

---

[4]   *Account*, Vol. 1, p.30.
[5]   *Account*, Vol. 1, p.30-1.

my mother's religious teachings, I shall have endless reason to bless my Maker.[6] She instructed her family in the Catechism which she had learned and the Bible, and taught her children to pray. Adam enjoyed the outdoor life from the age of six and he took a great interest in horsemanship, swimming and fishing. He enjoyed sports and he was a master at weightlifting and balancing. The young Adam was skilled in the latter game, where almost anything might be balanced in the hands, including ladders, sledgehammers and crowbars.

Adam's progress at school was very slow and his father put him to study Lily's Latin Grammar and taught him to read. This was new and painful and the more he tried, he could not commit to memory. The more the class progressed Adam couldn't follow them - and at last, he took up an English Testament and made his way into an English class. The master saw his ruse and said, 'Sir, what brought you here? Where is your Latin Grammar?' He burst into tears and said, 'I cannot learn it.' The master replied, 'Go, Sir, and take up your Grammar. If you do not speedily get that lesson, I shall pull your ears as long as Jowler's [a large dog belonging to the premises] and you shall be a beggar till the day of your death.'[7] These were terrible words and they struck home to Adam. He retired and sat down beside a fellow pupil – where he was received with the bitter taunts: 'What, have you not learned the lesson yet? O, what a stupid ass! You and I began together: you are now only in *As in praesenti* and I am in syntax!'[8]

The outcome was extraordinary and it is revealing that Adam Clarke retold his experience (in the third person) in his autobiographical memoirs.

> The effect of this was astonishing. Young Clarke was roused as from a lethargy; he felt, as he expressed himself, as if something had broken within him: his mind in a moment was all light. Though he felt indescribably mortified, he did not feel indignant: what, said he in himself, shall I ever be a dunce, and the butt of those fellow's insults? He snatched up his book, in a few moments committed the lesson to memory; got the construction speedily, went up and said it, without missing a

[6]   James Everett, *Adam Clarke Portrayed* (3 vols.; London: Hamilton, Adams, and Co., 1843-1849), Vol. 1, p.15; hereafter cited as 'Everett'.
[7]   Tracy, p.13.
[8]   *Account*, Vol. 1, p.33.

word; took up another lesson, acquired it almost immediately, said this also without a blemish, and in the course of that day wearied the master with his so often repeated returns to say lessons, and committed to memory all the Latin verses with their English construction, in which heavy and tedious Lily has described the four conjugations with their rules. Nothing like this had ever appeared in the school before. The boys were astonished, admiration took the place of mockeries and insult, and from that hour, it may be said from that moment, he found his memory at least capable of embracing every subject that was brought before it, and his long sorrow was turned into instant joy![9]

That is what Dr. Clarke thought about the outcome and it is difficult not to be persuaded by it. Up to that time he felt mortified and how he describes it might well have been the case. It turned Adam Clarke into a scholar and made him a lifetime student of scripture.

In the year 1777 Methodist preachers visited the parish in which the Clarkes lived. Adam Clarke went to hear them, and the first Methodist preacher he heard was John Brettell, who was preaching in a barn. Clarke did not remember the text or the sermon but he did remember that Brettell had announced that no matter what the Westminster Confession said, the Bible teaches present salvation from all sin. Later, an Irish Methodist preacher Thomas Barber (born in Co Fermanagh in 1751), began preaching over the whole region, using schools, barns, houses and the open air. The Clarke family heard him, took him in to their home and approved of his doctrine. Adam went to every service, and this, together with personal counsel from Brettell, soon created a seeking spirit, and so he began to seek present salvation.

Clarke began attending the Methodist Society meetings and Andrew Hunter of Coleraine spoke to him about giving his young heart to God. These words pierced Adam to the heart and divine conviction persisted day and night. In 1778 he went to work in a field which his father owned between Portstewart and Coleraine. Adam Clarke (writing in the third person) gives details of his own experience:

> One morning, in great distress of soul, he went out to his work in the field. He began but could not proceed, so great was his mental anguish. He fell down on his knees on the earth and prayed but seemed to be

[9]   *Account*, Vol. 1, pp.33-34.

without power or faith. He arose and endeavoured to work but could not.... His faith in the atonement, so far as it concerned himself, was almost entirely gone.... He had not God's approbation.... even the words of prayer at last failed; he could neither plead nor wrestle with God.... It is said the time of man's extremity is the time of God's opportunity. He now felt, 'Come to the holiest through the blood of Jesus.' He looked up, confidently to the Saviour of sinners. His agony subsided, his soul became calm. A glow of confidence thrilled through his frame and guilt and condemnation were gone.... He sat down upon the ridge where he had been working, full of ineffable delight. He praised God. His physical strength returned and he felt a sudden transition from darkness to light.... O, what a change was here![10]

Adam's testimony quickly became a burning and shining light and he went from village to village and shared his faith. His method was to call at a home and ask if he could have prayer with the family. The answer was invariably 'yes', and then he asked if they would like to invite any neighbours to join with them. When all had gathered, he would read Scripture, lead hymn singing, talk about religion, the awfulness of sin, and then lead the group in prayer, before moving on to another such service. His conversion soon transformed the family life at the Clarke home and he soon was the leader of devotions for the nine members of his family and they became members of the Methodist connexion. Adam Clarke was now nearing the age of twenty and his parents wanted him to become a Church of Ireland minister or a medical doctor like his older brother Tracy. However, the family now had little money and it was finally decided that Adam should go into business. He was sent as an apprentice to Francis Bennett of Coleraine, who owned an Irish linen business. He got on well in his work until one day he and Mr. Bennett were dealing with a piece of linen and they found that it did not stretch far enough. 'Lay hold on that piece and.... we'll soon make it come up to the yard,' urged Mr. Bennett. Adam was sure it wouldn't stretch and he refused to lay hold of it. Mr. Bennett was sure it would but he couldn't persuade Adam to touch that linen. After a while both men gave up

---

[10] *Account*, Vol. 1, pp.99-102.

and it was plain to Adam that he could not carry on and after this event he left.[11]

About this time he became acquainted with Mr. John Bredin, one of the Methodist preachers on the Londonderry circuit. Bredin made him an occasional helper on the circuit and urged him to preach. Although Adam had exhorted many times, he had never taken a text and preached. This was a sacred and fearful thing to him. Finally he yielded, and at the village of New Buildings (a few miles south of the city of Londonderry) on June 19, 1779, he preached his first sermon from the text, 'We know that we are of God, and the whole world lieth in wickedness' (1 John 5:19). During the next two weeks by popular demand he preached five more times, and a new vocation loomed before him. The call was confirmed when the verse was strongly impressed upon him which reads, 'Ye have not chosen me but I have chosen you, and ordained you, that ye should go and bring forth fruit' (John 15:16).

Clarke was now convinced that the Lord wanted him to serve in the Methodist Circuit but he was afraid what his parents would say. When he mentioned it to them, his mother fumed and said he would bring divine curses. 'We have brought you up with much care and trouble; your brother is gone, your father cannot last always, you should stay with your family and labour and support those who have so long supported you, and not go to be a fugitive and vagabond over the face of the earth.'[12] Adam was in a dilemma and prayer was his only refuge and he left for Coleraine on business. When he returned his mother was entirely changed in her attitudes and she and Adam's father were in one mind and they made way for him to go. When he reached Londonderry he found Mr. Bredin waiting, with a letter from John Wesley, but not himself able to travel. So on Saturday, August 17, 1782, Adam sailed alone for England, breaking away from family connections, and going on the authority of a divine command, but not knowing what was in store.

---

[11] Samuel Dunn, *Christian Theology by Adam Clarke.... with a Life of the Author by Samuel Dunn*, [1835], p.12; hereafter cited as 'Dunn'.
[12] Tracy, p.21.

Adam arrived at Kingwood School (near Bristol) a week later and handed the headmaster, Mr. Simpson, the letter from John Wesley. Simpson told him that he knew nothing of his coming and Mr. Wesley was away and would not be back for two weeks. Reluctantly Simpson told him that they had only one spare room but without any heat or bedding, and that Adam would have to stay there but he would not be permitted to attend classes, chapel or meals and his food and water would be brought to him by a servant. He soon discovered the reason for his isolation. He was Irish and they all supposed he might have the itch! He was informed that by rubbing himself with Jackson's Itch Ointment eventually he might come down with the rest of his class. Adam was desperate.

> Early refuge I had none. It is utterly impossible for me to describe the feelings, I may justly say the agony of my mind.... In this state, smelling worse that a polecat, I tumbled with a heavy heart and streaming eyes into my worthless bed. The woman that brought me bread and milk for breakfast - for dinner - and for supper - for generally I had nothing else, and not enough of that - I begged her to let me have a clean pair of sheets. It was in vain: no clean clothes of any kind were afforded me; I was left to make my own bed, sweep my own room and empty my own basin. For more than three weeks no soul performed any kind act for me.[13]

Adam had no money and he was put to work in the gardens - and the result was startling. He worked in the school garden and one day he dug up a gold half-guinea coin. He gave it to the headmaster, Mr. Simpson but he refused it, saying it wasn't his. He asked Adam to keep it until an inquiry was made. The next day he heard that the English teacher, Mr. Cornelius Bayley, had lost a half-guinea, so he gave the coin to him. Three days later Mr. Bayley returned the half-guinea to Adam, saying that although he had indeed lost such a coin, he could not be sure that it was this one and he could not conscientiously keep it. When Adam protested, Mr. Bayley was adamant. 'I will not keep it. I have been uneasy in my mind since I took it.'[14] The young Adam Clarke suddenly found himself comparatively rich. He had arrived in Bristol almost penniless and now he owned half a guinea, more money

---

[13] *Account*, Vol. 1, pp.154-156.
[14] *Account*, Vol. 1, pp.163-164.

than he had ever had, and the equivalent of more than a month's wages in 1782.

What Adam Clarke did with that half-guinea was to prove momentous. He could justifiably have spent it on food and clothing but it was not on such necessities that the money was spent. Bayley was about to publish his Hebrew Grammar (*An Entrance into the Sacred Language*) and Adam paid more than half the money to order a copy. What a decision that proved to be! It allowed him to teach himself Hebrew, and from that simple beginning his immense accumulation of biblical learning gradually developed. Having mastered Hebrew, eventually came Adam Clarke's greatest published achievement - his *The Holy Bible with a Commentary and Critical Notes.* Recalling the half-guinea incident shortly before his death in 1832, Clarke wrote: 'I purchased Mr. Bayley's Hebrew Grammar by which work I acquired a satisfactory knowledge of that language, which ultimately led me to read over the Hebrew Bible. Had I not got that Grammar, I probably should never have turned my mind to Hebrew learning and most certainly have never written a *Commentary* on Divine Revelation. Behold how great a matter a little fire kindleth!'[15]

When John Wesley finally arrived in Bristol, Adam couldn't wait to see what the Methodist leader had for him.

> I went into Bristol, saw Mr. Rankin, who carried me across to Mr. Wesley's study, off the great lobby of the rooms over the chapel in Broadmead. He tapped at the door which was opened by this truly apostolic man. Mr. Rankin retired. Mr. Wesley took me kindly by the hand and asked me how long since I had left Ireland. Our conversation was short. He said, 'Well, brother Clarke, do you wish to devote yourself entirely to the work of God?' I answered, 'Sir, I wish to do and be what God pleases.' He then said, 'We want a preacher for Bradford (Wilts.); hold yourself in readiness to go thither; I am going into the country, and will let you know when you shall go.' He then turned to me, laid his hands upon my head, and spent a few moments in praying to God to bless and preserve me, and to give me success in the work to which I was called.[16]

---

15 *Account*, Vol. 1, p.164.
16 *Account*, Vol. 1, p.165.

Adam Clarke was now ready to be launched into the Methodist Circuit and he longed for the opportunity to be used and led by the Lord.

Circuit and Literary Pursuits

Essentially Clarke had no other book but the Bible, and the habit of prayer was his continual exercise. He read the Bible often upon his knees and often watered it with his tears. He never entered the pulpit without prayer and he longed to see what was the difference prayer and study made when he faced the people week after week. He knew that he had the rudiments of literature and an insatiable thirst for knowledge, especially the knowledge of God and his works. Such were the qualifications of Adam Clarke when he set out on September 27, 1782, to minister to the people called Methodists.

His first circuit was in Bradford, Wiltshire, where he stayed for eleven months. He was anxious to improve his sermons, and so preaching every day suited him. The village of Road (near Trowbridge) was in his circuit and he first arrived there in the spring of 1783. The congregations here were very small and reports had gone out that a little boy was to preach in the Methodist chapel this coming Sunday. When Adam arrived the place was crowded with young people, all eager to see and hear the young preacher. Perhaps the Methodists seldom called young preachers for Adam was nearing twenty-three. In many parts the work of the circuit prospered, and when Clarke visited again several years later he found the work was still flourishing. While visiting the societies, his *Hebrew Grammar* reached him and he was soon enjoying reading it through and through. This *Grammar* precluded him from purchasing a Hebrew Bible, but the *Grammar* introduced him to the laying out of Hebrew sentences. The lessons and analytical parts are good but the rest of the work is imperfect. In his Latin, Greek and French, he couldn't make progress and laid it aside for a time. Adam Clarke took up other reading and so introduced himself to the history of the church by reading *A Concise Ecclesiastical History*, based on John Wesley's abridgement of Maclaine's English translation of the Swedish scholar John Lawrence Moshheim's original voluminous Latin work. Clarke worked at improving his French by reading Abbé Maury's *Discours sur V*

Eloquence de la Chaire, 'A Discourse on Pulpit Eloquence'. Struck with what he found, Adam wrote a piece hoping John Wesley might consider it for publication in the *Arminian Magazine.* Wesley writing to Clarke on February 3, 1786, invited him to send his translation: 'You should not forget French or anything you have learned. I do not know whether I have read the book you speak of; you may send your translation at your leisure. Be all in earnest, and you shall see greater things than these.'[17] Wesley must have liked Clarke's translation because it was later printed in the magazine. Adam also considered Wesley's advice to be of the highest authority, believing it to be next only to the divine oracles. Accordingly, during the same year Adam read Wesley's *Letter on Tea* and never again once tasted tea or coffee until his death.[18] Curiously, Wesley (on medical advice) after having left off the use of tea or coffee, later took it up again about twelve years after publishing his 'Letter to a Friend', but Adam never practiced tea drinking again.

In August 1783 Adam Clarke was appointed to a large circuit centred at Norwich. With him there were three men, and Clarke gave one whole week per month to Norwich and three weeks to visiting the country. The following year when John Wesley visited the county, Adam had the joy of hearing him preach twice a day for the week. At the end of the week, on Saturday, October 25, 1783, writing of Mr. Wesley, Clarke made the following entry in his *Journal:*

> Here, I took my farewell of this precious servant of God. O, Father, let thy angels attend him wheresoever he goes; let the energetic power of thy Spirit accompany the words he shall speak, and apply them to the hearts of all that shall hear them, and may there be the means of conviction, conversion, comfort, and strength, to all, as they may severally require. And let me also abundantly profit by the things I have heard from him.[19]

---

[17] John Wesley, *Letters,* (ed. John Telford; 8 vols; London: Epworth Press, 1931), Vol. 7, p.314; hereafter cited as 'Wesley, *Letters'.*

[18] John Wesley, *A Letter to a Friend Concerning Tea* (London: W. Strahan, 1748), reprinted in *Works* (3rd Edn; 14 vols.; ed. Thomas Jackson; London: Wesleyan Methodist Bookroom, 1872); Vol. 11, p.504-515.

[19] *Account,* Vol. 1, p.207.

Adam Clarke's religious experience was the work of God's Holy Spirit in the soul, and while he was in the Norwich Circuit he wrote to John Wesley and told him that when he was in Trowbridge, the Holy Spirit impressed on him the need for entire sanctification.

> Since I was justified, I have expected and prayed for the inestimable blessing of a heart in all things devoted to God; which, soon after I received pardon, I found to be indispensable necessary. But, meeting with little encouragement, I obtained it not.... I continued in this state till I came to this kingdom, when you ordered me into the Bradford Circuit. Here the good Lord was pleased to give me a sight of the unspeakable depravity of my heart.... I had become acquainted with a good man, a local preacher, who was a partaker of this precious privilege, and from him I received some encouragement and direction in the quest of it. He encouraged me to seek it with all my strength and believe in the ability and willingness of my God to accomplish the great work. Soon after, while wrestling in prayer, and endeavouring, self-desperately, to believe, I found a change wrought in my soul, which I endeavoured through grace to maintain amid grievous temptations…. My indulgent Saviour continued to support…. me, and enabled me with all my power to preach the glad tidings to others.[20]

Adam Clarke kept these sanctifying graces all his life, and for another forty-eight years, he was 'in the spirit' and never lost what God had given him at Trowbridge.

On Saturday, August 28, 1784, he reached St. Austell Circuit in Cornwall and through the preaching of Francis Wrigley, William Church and Adam Clarke the Methodists grew in number. Among those who joined the Methodists Society at this time was Samuel Drew (1765-1833) who shortly after terminated his apprenticeship to a shoemaker to become a local preacher. A man of remarkable genius and learning, Drew showed great ability in reaching men and women for Christ and in later years he served as a secretary to Adam Clarke. He was the first to make his name in philosophy and wrote the *Identity and Resurrection of the Human Body* (1809) and B*eing and Attributes of Deity* (1811). The work in this circuit was demanding, and although his popularity with the people was great, at times he felt at times like

---

[20] J.W. Etheridge, *The Life of the Rev. Adam Clarke, LL.D.* (3rd edn; London: John Mason, 1858), pp.402-3 and pp.415-6; hereafter cited as 'Etheridge'.

giving up. It was then that he met with the rarest gift from heaven, a true friend, Richard Mabyn from Camelford. Mabyn watched over Adam's needs and Mrs. Mabyn treated him as their dear friend. Adam Clarke was always welcome in their home, and their friendship lasted until the end of Mabyn's life in 1820, long after Clarke had left the circuit.

In August 1785 Adam Clarke was moved to the Plymouth Dock Circuit and his colleagues were John Mason and John King. The three men laboured together and the whole circuit saw revival. It was during this engagement that Adam revised his studies, and to help him, a naval officer, James Hore, lent Adam his two folio volumes of *Chambers' Encyclopaedia*. Adam spent many months in going through this and noting down its findings, commenting that 'I owe more to Mr. Hore, than to most men, for the loan of this work. The gift of a thousand indiscriminate volumes would not have equaled the utility of this loan.'[21] To aid him in his Hebrew studies he had purchased Edward Leigh's *Critica Sacra*, (1662 edition) a substantial compilation which not only gave him the literal sense of all Greek and Hebrew words in the Old and New Testaments but also adds enriching philological and theological notes to each definition. Clarke was also helped at Plymouth by a Miss Kennicott, the sister of the Hebrew scholar Benjamin Kennicott (1718-1783), who loaned him a copy her late brother's major two-volume edition of the Hebrew Bible (*Vetus Testamentum hebraicum cum variis lectionibus*), which details all the then known Hebrew biblical texts. Adam spent many hours studying this subject, and it gave him his first knowledge of Biblical Criticism.

As the Conference drew nearer, there was a strong desire to have Adam Clarke appointed to Plymouth for a second year, but Robert Brackenbury (1752-1818), who had been sent by Wesley to the Channel Islands in 1783, sent word that he needed a preacher in Jersey who was capable of understanding French. To this end Clarke was ordered to sail with Brackenbury. In the meantime Adam had visited his brother, Tracy Clarke, then a surgeon, living at Magull, near Liverpool. As Brackenbury was still not ready to sail, Adam decided

---

[21]   *Account*, Vol.1, p.230.

to pay a short visit to see Mr. Knapp and other friends at his old circuit at Trowbridge. Here he renewed his acquaintance with the three Cooke sisters Mary, Elizabeth and Frances; and from this a closer friendship began which resulted two years later in the marriage of Adam and Mary. Eventually, Brackenbury was ready and Adam sailed with him from Southampton, and arrived at Brackenbury's house at St Helier, Jersey on October 26, 1786. After a short time, it was agreed that Adam would move on to develop the work in Guernsey. Being stationed on a small island meant he had little long distance travelling to do, and being cut off from direct contact with former acquaintances meant that Adam was able to get down to the serious study of Greek and Latin. He then turned his mind to the Septuagint to find out how it differed from the Hebrew text and the hard work of these translation studies benefitted him for the rest of his life. Later, he was able to visit other societies on the islands, and discovered that the public library at St. Helier contained a large collection of excellent books. It was here that Clarke found a copy of the rare six-volume 'Polyglot Bible' (*Biblia sacra polyglotta*, edited by Bishop Brian Walton, London, 1654-7). With this, and having already used a copy of Walton's *Introductio ad Linguas Orientales*, Clarke was able to apply himself closely to the Syriac and then by collating the original texts in the Polyglot, he found the Hebrew, Samaritan, Chaldee, Syriac, Vulgate and Septuagint. Adam felt the need of his own Polyglot Bible. On receiving a letter with a £10 bank note, he wrote to a friend in London who managed to buy him a copy for just ten pounds, but still far above his then total income of three pounds a quarter. Adam Clarke saw the hand of God in this provision of both Bayley's Hebrew Grammar (at Kingswood school) and now Walton's *Polyglotta*, which in turn provided him with the basic tools fundamental to his eventually becoming an internationally recognized scholar of oriental languages and Biblical Literature.

From the Channel Islands, Adam recorded a story concerning John Wesley and a remarkable answer to prayer. In the year 1787 John Wesley, accompanied by Thomas Coke and Joseph Bradford, visited the Channel Islands and preached to large congregations in Jersey and Guernsey. Having made preparations to be in Bristol on a particular day, Wesley set sail for Southampton, with Adam Clarke. They were obliged to make frequent tacks in order to clear the island. John Wesley was reading in his cabin and he put his head above deck and enquired what was the matter. The sailors told him that the wind was contrary and Mr. Wesley said, 'Then let us go to prayer.' Thomas Coke, Joseph Bradford and Adam Clarke went to prayer and as soon as they had ended, John Wesley broke out into fervent supplication.

> Almighty and everlasting God, thou hast sway every where, and all things serve the purposes of thy will: thou holdest the winds in thy fists, and sittest upon the water floods, and reignest a King for ever: command these winds and these waves that they obey Thee; and take us speedily and safely to the haven whither we would be.[22]

Adam Clarke went on deck and was amazed to find the vessel now sailing steadily on, soon to be anchored safely in at its original destination, Penzance Bay. Mr. Wesley made no special remark because he believed that God heard such prayers. In his *Journal* for the September 6, 1787, Wesley simply reports: 'In the morning, Thursday 6, went on board with a fair, moderate wind. But we had but just entered the ship when the wind died away. We cried to God for help, and it presently sprung up, exactly fair, and did not cease till it brought us into Penzance Bay.'[23]

Adam Clarke aged 27

Clarke travelled from Cornwall with Wesley as far as Bristol, but then went on to Trowbridge to meet with Mary Cooke. Despite some opposition, Adam Clarke and Mary were later married, on April 17, 1788. It was to be a union of the highest order lasting until Adam died in 1832. The Clarke's eventually had six sons and six daughters, but

---

[22] *Account*, Vol. 1, p.259.
[23] John Wesley, *Works* (Bicentennial Edition; projected 35 vols.; Oxford: Oxford University Press, 1975-1983 & Nashville: Abingdon Press, 1984-), Vol. 24, p.57 hereafter cited as 'Wesley, *Works* [BE] '.

three of their sons and three of their daughters died in infancy. Adam was stationed at Guernsey until July 1789, when with his wife Mary and their baby son, they travelled to Trowbridge. Here Clarke left his family while he went on to the Conference in Leeds, where he received an appointment to the Bristol Circuit. Adam soon found that Bristol had several good libraries, as well as providing opportunity to add to his own library by visits to numerous second-hand bookshops. Henry Moore (1751-1844), paid tribute to Adam Clarke at this period.

> I met him in Bristol. I was glad to see a considerable alteration in his person. I found he had been a hard student and had made progress, especially in Oriental literature. His library alarmed me. He had among his other works a Polyglot Bible and he seemed determined to master every tongue in it. I said, 'Brother Clarke, you have got a choice collection of books, but what will you do with them? As a Methodist preacher, you cannot give them that attention which they demand.' He smiled and said, 'I will try.' I found he had been trying indeed. To an improvement in Latin, Greek, and French, he had added a considerable knowledge of Hebrew; and he showed me a Chaldee Grammar which he had written out, in order to be able to study the whole of the prophet Daniel. As he had not hitherto been appointed to Circuits favourable to such studies, I was surprised at the advancement he had made.... But I found my friend had not neglected this high calling ['to save souls.... and be spent therein']. His discourses seldom smelled of the lamp, and he was zealous for the Lord.[24]

In 1790 the Conference was held in Bristol and with Clarke's health not being good, he was advised to use the waters at Buxton as a means of recovery. He tried the waters both by drinking and bathing and had his health completely restored. For two years he resided in Manchester and the work of God prospered. For the next two years he laboured in Liverpool and was due to preach at what was then a small village called Aintree. After preaching they were on their way home when two men waylaid him and threw a stone which caused a large wound on Adam's head. Dr. Tracy Clarke was with him and examined him in a cottage, determined that he should not be moved. The next day Adam was moved to Dr. Tracy Clarke's home and the day after to Adam's own home. In the summer of 1794 Adam's parents removed

---

[24]   Etheridge, p.263.

from Ireland and settled in Manchester where his father obtained a living in a grammar school. During his two years of residence, John Pawson (1737-1806) and Adam Clarke had the satisfaction of seeing the Society more than doubled and the Lord blessed their services.

At the close of the 1795 Conference, Adam was transferred to London where he spent the next three years. Here he began to write his *Commentary* on the Old and New Testaments. He began a critical reading of the original texts, and he translated every verse of the Old and New Testaments and compared them with the Authorized Version. He was also diligently pursuing his oriental studies in order for a better understanding of Oriental poetry and diction. He did not finish the *Commentary* until April 17, 1826, a period of thirty-one years. He had laboured at the task for three decades and now it was finished and was offered to the public. On pages to follow, we will consider this work very carefully.

In the year 1797 Adam Clarke published a pamphlet, *A Dissertation on the Use and Abuse of Tobacco*.[25] The pages are replete with botanical, medical and historical information, and it offers a warning against all those who use tobacco for pleasure. One of the preachers at the 1805 Conference got up and told what the effects of reading it were: 'My wife and I used tobacco for between thirty and forty years. When I read Mr. Clarke's pamphlet I was convinced that I should give it up: I did so, and so did my wife; I then recommended it to the society.... All who read the pamphlet gave it up.'[26] Eventually it became the rule that no preachers should be admitted to full connection until they had given up smoking.

In the summer of 1798 Adam Clarke and his family moved from London to the Bristol Circuit. Adam was disturbed at the state of his father and would have visited him but his own health prevented it. He wrote to John Berwick, in Manchester, begging him to look after his father and mother. Berwick wrote back, stating that John Clarke had passed into eternity:

---

[25] *Account*, Vol. 2, p.22.
[26] Everett, Vol. 2, p.180.

This forenoon I found a desire to go and see your father. When I arrived they were just going to send for me.... He was seated in his chair but wanted to be removed into bed.... After he had written those few words he was got into bed and appeared better.... I had spoken much to him respecting you: I told him I thought it well you had not been sent for as you could have done him no good. He said 'he was perfectly satisfied, for if you had suffered from the effects of the journey he should have been very unhappy.' He added that 'he had no pain, and that one moment in eternity would compensate for all he had suffered here.'.... At my return I found he had just gone to glory, without a groan.[27]

On the same sheet of paper Berwick had included Adam's father's note, it read as follows: 'May the blessing of God, and a dying father's blessing, ever be upon you all, my children. I die full of hope and happy. JOHN CLARKE. God bless you all. Adam,=Mary. William,=Mary. Tracy - all - all. Amen.'[28] Adam sent for his widowed mother and she stayed with him until he moved from Bristol; only then did she go to stay with her daughter, Mrs. Exley, who was settled in Bristol. Adam's father was buried in Ardwick churchyard in Manchester and on his tombstone were inscribed these words. 'Here lieth the body of John Clarke, M.A., who departed this life, Nov. 2d, 1798, in the 62d year of his age.'[29]

In the year 1800 Adam Clarke translated into English a French translation of an original German work by Christoph Christian Sturm (1740-1786). Collating it with the German, Clarke published it as *Reflection on the Works of God in Nature and Providence for every day of the year*. Its rapid sale proved to be one of Clarke's most popular editions. For some time before this he had been contemplating beginning his own *Commentary* on the Bible, but he lacked access to a good Arabic Dictionary. He wrote to a bookseller to procure one for him. A copy had just become available but the bookseller said he would have to ask forty-eight guineas. Adam was in a dilemma. He immediately wrote to Mr. Ewer of Bristol, promising that within three months the sums would be paid. Mr. Ewer replied and enclosed the

---

27   *Account*, Vol. 2, pp.35-6.
28   *Account*, Vol. 2, pp.36-7.
29   *Account*, Vol. 2, p.37.
18

money, and Adam sent it to the bookseller. He had found a rare copy of Franciscus Meninski's four-volume Turkish-to-Latin dictionary and grammar *Linguarum Orientalium* (1680), which was to be his constant study companion for the remainder of his life; the loan was repaid within the promised period.

In 1802 Clarke edited and published, *A Bibliographical Dictionary containing a Chronological Account of the most curious, scarce, useful and important books in all departments of literature, which have been published in Latin, Greek, Coptic, Hebrew, Samaritan, Syriac, Chaldee, Ethiopic, Arabic, Persian, and Armenian.* To these he added, *An Account of the best English Translations of each Greek and Latin Classic.* This work was originally published in six volumes and to that he added in the year 1806, two volumes, *Bibliographical Miscellany.* About the same time he published a small work, entitled, *A Succinct Account of Polyglot Bibles, from the publication of that by Porrus in the year 1516, to that of Reineccius in 1750.* Adam also published an account of the Greek New Testament, *A Succinct Account of the principal Editions of the Greek Testament, from the first printed in Complutum, in 1514, to that by Professor Griesbach, in 1797.* These works contain a mass of information and guide a student into an overview of Biblical literature. As well as tracking down the very latest Bible production, Dr. Clarke was busy in Methodist work and changing his place of service every few years.

After three years in Bristol, the Conference directed Adam Clarke to the Liverpool Circuit, where he stayed for the next three years, from 1801 to 1803. Immediately he threw himself into work, and on both Sundays and weekdays he found himself preaching. In order to cultivate learning about literature and science for himself and others, Clarke set about forming a Society, first producing its printed rules: *Rules of the Philological Society.* Both the Rules and Questions were chosen by Adam Clarke and he was elected its President. The Society produced many excellent papers on scientific knowledge and useful philosophy.

While he was in Liverpool the death of his brother affected Adam greatly. In the forty-fifth year of his age Tracy Clarke died, and Adam saw that consumption was mostly the cause. From childhood Tracy and he had been lifelong companions and it was a wrench to see him taken from him. Many times Adam thought of their working together on their father's farm; one would go to school and the other would carry on the farm. On seeing his brother sinking fast, Adam wrote the following in his pocket-book. 'Sept. 6, 1806. I went to see my dying brother: he is in a very happy state of mind.... Sept. 20. I attended the remains of my precious brother to the earth in Melling Church-yard, Lancashire.'[30]

From 1803 to 1805, Adam Clarke was sent to the Manchester Circuit and from five to seven in the morning, he taught Hebrew and Greek to young men, and as a result, about four of them entered the ministry. From a manuscript (written in 1832) by Clarke, the origin of *The Strangers' Friend Society* may be learned.

> The Strangers' Friend Society was formed by the Rev. Mr. John Wesley and myself in Bristol in the year 1789, on the foundation of a small meeting, the members of which subscribed one penny per week for the relief of the poor.... I went the next year, 1790, to Dublin and there I formed a Society of the same name.... From Dublin I went to Manchester and formed another Society.... I went from Manchester to Liverpool and formed a similar Society there.... In 1795 I removed to London and formed at Wapping the Strangers' Friend Society.... It died a natural death... The name 'Benevolent' was afterwards used, I believe, first in City Road... This is the simple truth in reference to the origin and formation of the Strangers' Friend Society.[31]

In 1804 Adam published a new edition of *Manners of the Ancient Israelites, containing an Account of their peculiar Customs, Ceremonies, Laws, Polity, Sects, Arts, and Trades*. This work is of great interest and gives an insight into their religious, civil and social polity. In addition he published a paper entitled, *A Succinct Account of the Principal Editions of the Greek Testament,* and another was *Observations on the Text of the Three Divine Witnesses, accompanied with a Plate containing two very correct Fac-Similes of 1 John v. 7, 8, and 9.*

---

[30] Etheridge, p.202, and *Account*, Vol. 2, p.68.
[31] *Account*, Vol. 2, p.73-4.

After remaining in Manchester for two years, the Wesleyan Conference directed Clarke to London and he went with his family to City Road. John Pawson (1737-1806) held Adam Clarke in very high esteem for they had been friends in London and Liverpool and they had borne the burden and heat of the day. The letter from Pawson is dated Wakefield, March 28, 1806.

> Oh, my Adam, my most affectionately beloved and esteemed friend and Brother, for whom God knoweth I ever had a sincere and most cordial regard, but now ten-fold more so then ever, I return you my sincerest and most cordial thanks for your kind invitation to me to come up to London, and to take up my abode at your house.... What I have experienced of the power, goodness, unmerited mercy, and love of God, during this affliction, is not to be described by me. Oh, the views, the soul-transporting views, of that heavenly felicity with which my soul hath been favoured. My loving friend, praise the name of the Lord with me, and for me; and you may tell all my beloved London friends, that John Pawson dies a witness of the saving power of those precious truths which have been taught and believed and experienced, among us from the beginning of Methodism.... Then thousand times ten thousand blessings attend you, your beloved Mary and all your family. John Pawson's dying prayer for you is, "That goodness and mercy may follow you all the days of your life, and that you dwell in the house of the Lord for ever".... Farewell for ever. Bless the Lord for me; and we shall all unitedly enjoy Him very soon. I am most affectionately and eternally, Yours in Christ Jesus.[32]

The Methodist Conference was held in Leeds this year and Adam Clarke was elected President. It was a signal honour to be elected President and Adam held the charge for a year. The newly-constituted British and Foreign Bible Society soon submitted his name and his biblical knowledge and Oriental studies constituted him a powerful auxiliary, and his brother-in-law, Joseph Butterworth, consulted him. Adam laboured to bring about a translation of the Scriptures into the Tartaric and Arabic languages and likewise into modern Greek. The time was approaching when Clarke would soon be removed from London and the British and Foreign Society wrote to the Methodist Conference asking them not to move Mr. Clarke. The Secretaries of

---

[32] *Account*, Vol. 2, pp.90-1.

the Methodist Conference wrote back, saying that Mr. Clarke would not be moved for another year.

There is one interesting example of Clarke's wider erudition that deserves to be better known. One of the prize exhibits in the Egyptian Gallery of the British Museum, London, is the Rosetta Stone. It was discovered at Rosetta by one of Napoleon's soldiers during the Egyptian Expedition of 1798, and later fell into the hands of the British. It has three inscriptions, one in Greek, one in hieroglyphics, and the third in characters that baffled the people that admired it. Dr. Clarke was requested to see the Stone and immediately pronounced it to be basalt, interspersed with mica and quartz. After examining the strange writing, he concluded: 'This is Coptic and differs only from the printing Coptic of Wilkin's Testament as printed Persian does from manuscript.'[33] Clarke's observations gave the key that eventually led to the translation.

Adam was allowed by the Methodist Conference to remain in London another year and by this time his literary character had brought him public notice. Professor Porson took note of his activities and voted to give Clarke his Diploma of M.A. Adam wrote to Professor Porson and thanked him for his suggestion:

> My dear Sir: It is only within a few hours that I have been informed of a request made to you by one of my friends for your recommendation to King's College, Aberdeen.... Not that I lightly esteem such honours; I believe them, when they are given through merit, next to those which come from God.... What you have said of me I know not, but I am satisfied you would not say nothing but what is kind and just; and to deserve and to have the smallest measure of the approbation of a man, who I am so fully satisfied stands eminently at the head of the Republic of Letters, would be to me, a very high gratification.[34]

On January 31, 1807, the University gave notice that 'this day unanimously conferred the degree of Master of Arts on Mr. Adam Clarke, Member of the Philological Society of Manchester and author of several literary works of merit.'[35]

---

[33] Etheridge, pp.270-271.
[34] *Account*, Vol. 2, pp.142-3.
[35] *Account*, Vol. 2, p.144.

In September of this year Adam Clarke produced the first volume of a work entitled, *A Concise Review of the Succession of Sacred Literature, in a Chronological Arrangement of Authors and their Works, from the invention of Alphabetical Characters to the year of our Lord 345*. In the spring of 1808 Adam had the honour of being presented with a Diploma of LL.D. from the University and King's College, Aberdeen. Adam Clarke thanked the Professor in a letter to him, stating:

> You will still, my dear Sir, lay me under greater obligation to yourself by receiving the expressions of my gratitude for your kindness, and by making similar acknowledge as acceptable as possible to your learned University. To add any thing to the respectability of King's College, though out of my power, will, notwithstanding, be an object of my sincere desire.[36]

In 1808 the attention of the House of Commons, London, was directed towards the condition of the Public Records. The principal archives of the more remote reigns of the English kings had been a hundred years before, collected and embodied in a series of twenty folios, under the title *Foedera*. Fourteen of these were edited by Thomas Rymer, an eminent antiquarian who held the office of Royal Historiographer and who died in 1713. The remaining six were edited by Robert Sanderson. There had been a large accumulation of public documents which were kept in various repositories together with a number of other valuable papers not included in the *Foedera*. Rymer had left a collection of folio volumes which, after his death, were taken into the possession of the government. To have these volumes arranged in the correct order was felt to be a duty of a country, and a commission was appointed to hand it to the right man. One preliminary was the appointment of a suitable editor and that was given to Dr. Adam Clarke and it will set a high estimate of the man chosen to whom the government and senate of England made their application. Clarke's own statement of this high office will serve to show it in his handwriting.

> Some time in February, 1808, I learned that I had had been recommended to His Majesty's commissioners of the public records, by the Right Hon. Charles Abbott, Speaker of the House of Commons, and

[36] *Account*, Vol. 2, pp.155-156.

one of his commissioners (to whom I was known only by some of my writings on bibliography) as a fit person to undertake the department of collecting and arranging those state papers which might serve to complete and continue Rymer's *Foedera*.... I was struck with surprise and endeavoured to excuse myself on the grounds of general unfitness.... At this the secretary smiled and said, 'Mr. Clarke, you will have the goodness to try; and meanwhile, pray, draw up the papers which the commissioners require, and I am ready to give you any assistance in my power.'[37]

His first task was to produce a report of the nature, number and localities of the materials which were to form the new supplement to the *Foedera*. It was an introductory lecture and it took the form of, *An Essay on the best mode of carrying into Effect a Compilation from unedited and latent Records, to form a Supplement.* Adam Clarke was able to furnish the requisite requirements and to quote the official minute:

> At a Board of the Commissioners appointed by His Majesty on the Public Records of the Kingdom, holden on Friday, 25 March, 1808, Present, the Rt. Hon. C. Abbott, Lord F. Campbell, Lord Redesdale, Lord Glenbervie, the bishop of Bangor, &c.; the secretary stated that Adam Clarke, LL.D., having been recommended on account of his extensive learning and indefatigable industry, as a fit person to revise and form a Supplement to Rymer's *Foedera* had prepared an essay and the secretary delivered in and the same was now read.[38]

Adam Clarke started a ten year contract with the government and he travelled around England and Ireland. He visited the antique records in the Tower, the Cottonian, Harleian, Landshown, and Sloan collections in the British Museum, as well as at the State Paper Office and the Rolls Chapel. The same work called him to the archives of various cathedrals, the Bodleian at Oxford, and the libraries of Corpus Christi and other Colleges at Cambridge and in Dublin, at Christchurch and the library at Trinity College. These labours, however, were oppressive and they occasioned Dr. Adam Clarke to write to the government-commission to be absolved from further service but did

---

[37] Etheridge, pp.305-6.
[38] Etheridge, pp.307-8.

not find release until 1819. He ended his service to the state by thanking God that he was able to give ten years to this service.

And here I register my thanks to God, the Fountain of wisdom and goodness, who has enabled me to conduct this most difficult and delicate Work for ten years, with credit to myself and satisfaction to His Majesty's Government. During that time I have been required to solve many difficult questions and illustrate many obscurities; in none of which have I ever failed, though the subjects were such as were by no means familiar to me, having little of an antiquarian and nothing of a forensic education.... The Work was to collect from all the archives of the United Kingdom, all authentic State Papers from the Conquest to the Accession of George III.... Many endeavoured to carp at the Work, but their teeth were broken in their attempt to gnaw the file.... To God only wise be glory and dominion, by Christ Jesus, for ever and ever. Amen. Millbrook, March 30, 1819.[39]

Dr. Adam Clarke heard that Mrs. Mabyn was dead and he wrote a letter to Mr. Maybn encouraging him to hold fast to the Lord. The letter is dated March 4th, 1811.

My very dear, and much respected Friend,

With that concern which becomes me as your friend, and which I should feel on the news of the death of one who long acted to me the part of a most tender and affectionate parent, I received the account of the death of your amiable partner. Though it was an event long expected, and indeed anticipated by all who were acquainted with the state of Mrs. Mabyn's health. I often feared that I should never have the privilege of seeing her before her death, and it has constituted a portion of my happiness, that I was thus favoured, and witness my friend dying in the Lord.... Now, my very dear friend, you must not abandon life, because God has taken away your partner: I mean, you must not be careless about life – you must take care of yourself: you may live many years, and do a little more for God's cause.... Will you come and see us? We will do every thing in the compass of our power, to make you comfortable.

With love to brothers and sisters Lobb, and all my friends in Camelford.

I am, my very dear friend,

Yours most affectionately,

A. Clarke.[40]

---

[39] *Account*, Vol. 2, pp.196-7.
[40] *Account*, Vol. 2, pp.249-251.

Coming home from a visit to Ireland in 1811, he found that his mother had died just before he could reach her. He called out, 'Is all well?' and the notice of his mother's death was what he found. He had loved his mother all during his life and he was devastated that she had gone. His mother taught them the Lord's Prayer, the Apostles' Creed, morning and an evening prayer, and the 23rd Psalm; every Lord's Day was strictly sanctified and she obliged them to hear the Church Catechism, and the Shorter Catechism. Adam Clarke was sure he never was converted unless he had heard his mother praying for him. A letter from the Rev. Thomas Roberts, the friend and neighbour of the departed, reveal all the respect he found for his colleague's mother.

> I am just informed that your good and esteemed mother has entered into life! She was one who most worthily shared my respect and regard; and for your consolation, I may truly say, you are justified in entertaining the best feelings when you reflect, that good Mrs. Clarke was your mother. She lived just so long, and died so well, as to leave in the heart of her son, nothing but acquiescence in the Divine will, and gratitude for that gracious dispensation of heaven which could not have been manifested in a manner more consolatory to the feelings of the man, the son, and a Christian.
> Adieu. I am,
> Your affectionate friend and brother,
> Thomas Roberts.[41]

Throughout these years Adam Clarke found it trying to be under obligation to the Wesleyan Methodists and at the beck and call of the literary world. It was partly on this account that Joseph Butterworth, his brother-in-law, found him an opening in the Librarianship of the Surrey Institution and he resided there for a year. He published, *A Narrative of the last Illness and Death of Richard Porson, M.A., Professor of Greek in the University of Cambridge. With a Fac-Simile of an Ancient Greek Inscription which was the Chief Subject of his last Literary Conversation.*[42]

On March 5, 1813, Dr. Clarke had the honour of being elected a Fellow of the Society of Antiquaries. This fellowship was to be highly gratifying and he had a high regard for it and it suited his peculiar

---

[41]   *Account*, Vol. 2, p.280.
[42]   *Account*, Vol. 2, p.199.

taste. A catalogue of books having been sent to him, he immediately looked it over and saw the first edition of Erasmus's Greek Testament for sale. On the following morning he went off and purchased the work. A few hours afterward Dr. Gossett went also to Paternoster Row but the book was gone. He called on Dr. Clarke and said, 'You have been very fortunate, Dr. Clarke, in having obtained this work, but how you got it before myself, I am at a loss to imagine, for I was at Bayne's directly after breakfast and it was gone.' 'But I was there before breakfast,' replied Dr. Clarke, 'and consequently, doctor, I forestalled you.'[43]

Clarke was elected President of the Conference and a general meeting was called in order to call attention of the public to missions in general, and it was held in City Road chapel and Dr. Clarke took the chair and delivered the address. The address was afterward published; *A short Account of the Introduction of the Gospel into the British Isles, and the obligation of Britons to make known its salvation to every nation of the earth.... by Adam Clarke, LL.D., F.A.S.* After many years in London, the Wesleyan Conference had him appointed to the Manchester Circuit, and Dr. Clarke must now be viewed in comparative retirement but at the Methodist Society in Manchester. He brought a property in Millbrook (not far from Liverpool), and made the journey to Manchester once a month.

On the May 10, 1818, Dr. Clarke received two Buddhist priests from on board a vessel at Blackwall on the Thames. He made them welcome and was surprised to see them handle English so well. Early in the morning they reported for religious instruction and two years later, on Sunday, May 7, 1820, Dr. Clarke baptized them in the name of the Trinity at the large Brunswick chapel in Liverpool. Adam Clarke wrote a letter of commendation for Adam Mundi Rathana and his cousin Alexander Dherma Rame:

....As they now intend to return to their own land, with the purpose of testifying to their benighted countrymen the gospel of the grace of God, I feel much pleasure in being able to recommend them to the notice of sincere Christians in general, wherever they may come; and especially to all who are in power and authority, both in ecclesiastical and civil

---

[43] *Account*, Vol. 2, p.319.

authority, being satisfied of their morality and loyalty to their principles, and that they are worthy of the confidence of all who may have any intercourse or connection with them.

Given under my hand, this 7th of May, 1820.

Adam Clarke.[44]

In the year 1821 Dr. Clarke was elected a member of the Royal Irish Academy on July 13, an honour particular to his feelings. This had come from Irish stock and he knew of some of the highest and the best in that country. In July the following year the Methodist Conference, which held its meeting in London, Adam Clarke was elected for the third time to be President. To have been chosen for a third time as President is unique in the annals of Methodism. In a letter to Dinah Ball, he had recorded the finishing of his *Memoirs of the Wesley Family*. In the Introduction, he gives thanks to 'his late excellent friend Miss Sarah Wesley, for her continual assistance; to the venerable and Reverend Thomas Steadman, Rector of St. Chad's, Shrewsbury.'[45] Although it is to John Wesley that he gives the most attention, these Memoirs close with the following. 'Such a family I have never read of, heard of, or known; nor, since the days of Abraham and Sarah, and Joseph and Mary of Nazareth, has there ever been a family to which the human race has been more indebted.'[46] With all his labours in so many fields, it is still more of a puzzle that *Memoirs of the Wesley Family* is not quoted in many John Wesley biographies. Writing biographies was not a pastime in which Adam Clarke excelled.

On January 4, 1823, Dr. Clarke was elected a *Member of the Geological Society of London*. Although he spent the chief part of his time at Millbrook, being deeply engaged in his notes on the *Commentary*, he preached normally on the Sunday either in Liverpool or chapels near his residence. In response to a letter from Sir Alexander Johnson, dated the February 1, 1823, he responded and was the original member of *An Asiatic Society in London*. His family had by now grown up and they all felt that Millbrook was too far away,

---

[44] *Account*, Vol. 2, pp.371-2.
[45] Adam Clarke, *Memoirs of the Wesley Family: Collected Principally from Original Documents* (London; J. Kershaw, 1823), p.xv; hereafter cited as 'Clarke, *Memoirs*'
[46] Clarke, *Memoirs, p.543.*

accordingly Dr. Clarke purchased land and a house at Eastcott, sixteen miles north from London, and in September 1824, he retired to it. There he shortly recovered his health and proceeded with his work on the *Commentaries* which was now drawing to a conclusion. There wasn't a place of worship within two miles of Haydon Hall, (the name of Dr. Clarke's house in Middlesex), so he opened one of his cottages for the purpose of preaching and it was soon filled with attentive hearers. As he owned such a house it was often the occasion of much good-humoured jesting, his colleagues jibing him that he could no longer join them in singing:
No foot of land do I possess
No cottage in the wilderness.[47]

Ill health now prevented Clarke continuing as a travelling preacher but there was no slacking on his amazing industry. His pen was never idle and he was also in great demand as a preacher. For eight years he and Mrs. Clarke lived in this house and it was eight years filled with excursions to the Shetland Islands, to England and to Ireland. Dr. Clarke was full of gracious dispositions and especially those of the household of faith. In all things he was a genuine catholic. He could say with Jerome: 'I am a Christian and the son of a Christian, bearing on my forehead the token of the Cross.' Names with him are next to nothing but there was one branch to which he was intimately united – Methodist. The Methodist people were his people and their God his God. Among them he was called, among them he lived, and laboured and, eventually, died.

Dr. Clarke was welcomed all over Britain but it was the people of the Shetland Isles who received a lot of his attention. On June 28, 1829, he wrote a letter to the Rev. Mr. Tabraham, desirous to get a labourer for these islands:
> My Dear Brother Tabraham, Long ago you were warmly recommended to me as a proper person for the Shetlands. I want you and your wife, in

---

[47] [Charles Wesley], Hymn 51, 'The Pilgrim', verse 6, in: *Hymns for those that seek and those that have Redemption in the Blood of Jesus Christ* (London: Printed by W. Strahan, 1747); repr. in *Poetical Works of John and Charles Wesley* (13 vols; ed. G. Osborn; London: Wesleyan-Methodist Conference Office, 1868-1872), Vol. 4, p.279; hereafter cited as *'Poetical Works'*.

the name of our Lord Jesus, to go to Lerwick and superintend the glorious work in those Islands: in no place under heaven perhaps can a faithful zealous minister of God have more fruit of his labours. I know the place, I know the people, I know the work, and I know the God who is there with His faithful workers. Had I twenty years less on my age, I would not write a leaf to entreat any person to go: I would go; I would there labour and there die, if it so pleased my Divine Master.... For the success of your work, scheme, labour, see that preachers spread themselves and everywhere mingle your labours; God will be with you. Set the people themselves to pray for the success of the gospel in all the Islands, and as concerns yourselves: watch for this, work for this, fast, pray, and believe for this.... Do not let me die before Dunrossness, Lunnasting, Sand, &c., chapels are built; with all my faith for Shetland, I do not see where money will be got, or how it can come, after the green sod covers me.... Oh! My Brothers, my dear Brothers in the Lord Jesus, my Brothers Tabraham, Stevenson, Bolam, M'Intosh, and Rickets, rush into every opening door, besiege the throne of endless mercy; make God your refuge and your strength: do not kill yourselves but spend and be spent for the souls in Shetland.... Hallelujah! Jesus is with you – fear not.[48]

Dr. Clarke attended the Wesleyan Conference held in Leeds in 1830, and the subject of 'negro slavery' was on everyone's lips and the Conference was asked to deal with it. The following Resolution was adopted:

> The Conference, taking into consideration the laudable efforts which are now making, to impress the public with a due sense of the injustice and inhumanity of continuing that system of slavery which exists in many of the colonies of the British Crown, invites a general application to Parliament, by petition, that such measures may in its wisdom be adopted as shall speedily lead to the universal termination of the wrongs inflicted upon so large a portion of our fellow-men.[49]

The Conference debated the subject warmly and drew up several strong resolutions enforcing the determinate opposition of the Methodists to the nefarious system of slavery. This opposition of the pastors in Methodism also placed their colleagues in opposition to it.

---

[48] *Adam Clarke*, 1833, Vol. 3, pp.201-3.
[49] Wesleyan Methodist Conference Minutes, Leeds 1830, cited in *Account*, Vol. 3, p.247.

Dr. Clarke was firmly in favour of the motion and speedy abolition and he wrote the following letter on the fly-leaf of a printed copy of the Resolution to his friends, Mr. and Mrs. Forshaw.

Dear Mr. and Mrs. Forshaw,

You will see from the preceding resolutions, what the Methodist ministers have done in a body, which is to be followed by petitions from every society and congregation in the United Kingdom, separately signed; and these will bring before the two houses of the legislature at least one million of names of honest men who are determined to use their preponderating influence in all the counties of England, to petition for the speedy and total abolition of colonial slavery.

There is no time now for trifling, or half measures. We have put our hands to the work, and by the help of God, we will do it with our might! Knowing that this will give pleasure to the benevolent heart which has long, and indeed successfully, laboured, to redress the great mass of wrong done in Africa, I send one of these tonight to Mr. Wilberforce.

I am, dear Mr. and Mrs. Forshaw,

Yours, very affectionately,

Adam Clarke.[50]

Dr. Clarke fulfilled his intention of sending a letter to Mr. William Wilberforce, as this reply to him from the great anti-slave campaigner shows:

Highwood Hill,
17th August, 1830.

My dear Dr. Clarke,

For you will permit me, I trust, to use the language of friendly regard, since I can truly assure you it is warranted abundantly by the undissembled feelings of my heart, I return you many thanks for your kind and highly gratifying communication. The 'Resolutions' are truly excellent; and I rejoice to hear that the cause of the poor slaves will be so zealously pleaded for you by your numerous congregations. With what insane, as well as wicked bitterness, are those most respectable men who are devoting themselves as missionaries to the service of God among the poor slaves in Jamaica, persecuted by the legislature of that island. In complaining of this ill usage, it would surely be useful to bring forward the testimony which has been borne to their disinterested

---

[50] *Account,* Vol. 3, p.248.

beneficence, and to the effects of their labours, in several of the other West-India islands....

Before I lay down my pen, which a complaint in my eyes permits me to use but very little, compared with the claims on it,.... let me express my regret that you were from home when Sergeant Pell and I paid our respects at Eastcott. We were received with great courtesy by Mrs. Clarke, and we saw many deeply interesting objects; but that which we most wished to see was absent. I hope I may be able some time or other to pay you another visit.... I am going from home very soon, but if it please God that we both live till another summer, I hope we may effect a meeting. Meanwhile, begging you to present my respects to Mrs. Clarke, I remain, with great respect and regard,

My dear Doctor,

Your obliged and faithful servant,

W. Wilberforce.[51]

About this time the interests of Dr. Clarke were drawn to whatever the venerable Mr. John Wesley had left, especially to those artists who had secured a just likeness of Wesley. On September 28, 1830, he received a letter from Samuel Manning.

Very dear Sir,

As I am already laid under such peculiar obligation to you for the important assistance rendered me in reference to the statue of Mr. Wesley, I should feel considerable hesitation in troubling you again on that subject, were it not for the encouragement you have given me to address you, after having been favoured with another visit from the president, and the Rev. Henry Moore, agreeable to your suggestion; and having received letters expressive of their approbation, since the alterations I had the pleasure to make by your direction. I beg to submit them for your consideration; and to say, that however flattering these testimonies may be, I am extremely anxious to avail myself of the recommendation you were so kind as to promise; and without which, I feel myself totally unable to proceed.

Waiting the favour of your reply at a convenience, I beg to remain, with great respect,

Dear Sir,

Your highly indebted and obedient servant,

Samuel Manning.[52]

---

[51] Letter of William Wilberforce (1759-1833) to Adam Clarke, see: *Account*, Vol. 3, pp.248-250.

Dr. Clarke replied by drawing up the annexed testimony of his approbation of Mr. Samuel Manning's statue of the Rev. John Wesley and also of the respective busts of the Founder of Methodism, taken by Enoch Wood of Burslem and Mr. John Forshaw of Liverpool.

September 30, 1830.

Few men in the British nation, have come more frequently under the hand of the artist than the late Rev. John Wesley.... Some were merely tolerable, and a very few true to nature and creditable to art. Mr. Enoch Wood, of Burslem, in 1781, made a model of Mr. Wesley, in busto, which was the most happily executed of all that had hitherto been done. Mr. Wesley himself was so satisfied that Mr. Wood would succeed in his work, though pressed by various duties, and straightened for time, he cheerfully sat five several times to this artist, till he was convinced that he had given a very faithful copy of nature. Some correct copies were taken from this model, and were spread among Mr. Wesley's intimate and original friends.... Fortunately the original model is still preserved: some years ago it was presented to me by the artist himself. This, to preserve it for ever, I had cast in brass.

I had the honour of Mr. Wesley's acquaintance for many years. I have been with him by night and by day, in the powerful exercises of his ministry, and of his mode of discipline, and this in troublous times; and I have seen and been with him in trials and dangers, by sea and by land: as his counsels can never be obliterated from my mind. The noble appearance of his face, I see in the *terra cotta* of Mr. Wood; and exactly transferred from it to the clay.... his attractive expression; in a word, his mind and his manner, as his friends now remaining, long beheld and rejoiced in him; and, as those, who have only seen him in his works, may be not a little glad to know on the faith of those who have seen him, and could judge, - I add, this is a perfect likeness of John Wesley.[53]

Dr. Clarke wrote to James Everett of Manchester on December 21, 'five o'clock a.m. Shortest Day in 1830'. Everett was a long-time

---

[52] *Account*, Vol. 3, pp.250-1; Samuel Manning ('the elder', 1786-1842) is the writer of this 1830 letter to Adam Clarke; but it was his son, Samuel Manning ('the younger', c. 1814-1866), who was the sculptor who, following his father's death, eventually made a life size marble statue of John Wesley (1849) for the Methodist Theological Institute at Richmond, Surrey.

[53] *Account*, Vol. 3, pp.251-3.

admirer of Adam Clarke and he compiled a life story, published 1843-1849.

> Dear Everett,
>
> In the name of God! Amen. About three-score and ten of such short days have I seen, and as my time in the course of nature, as it is called, is now ended, I need to have little to do, as my age is at the longest, and this day is the shortest I may ever see; yet I have never fallen out with life. I have borne many of its rude blasts, and I have been fostered with many of its finest breezes; and should I complain against time and the dispensations of Providence, than shame would be to me!.... Therefore my grand object in all my best and most considerate moments, is, to live to get good from God, that I may do good to my fellows; and this alone is the way in which man can glorify his Maker.... It is in and through the Almighty Jesus alone, that the all-binding, all-persuading, all-constraining, and all-pervading love of God to man, was ever known.... Jesus the Christ incarnated; Jesus the Christ crucified; Jesus the Christ dying for our offences, and rising again for our justification; Jesus sending forth the all-pervading, all-refining, and all-purifying light and energy of His Holy Spirit, has revealed the secret, and accomplished the purpose of that God whose name is mercy and whose name is love.
>
> O, thou incomprehensible Jehovah, thou eternal Word, thou ever-enduring and all-pervading Spirit; Father, Son and Holy Ghost, in the plenitude of thy eternal Godhead, in thy light, I, in a measure, see Thee; and in thy condescending nearness to my nature, I can love Thee, for Thou hast loved me.... O, my Everett, here am I fixed, here am I lost, and here I find my God.... When I sit down to write, not one word of what is written was designed. I only intended to write a little on a subject in which you had so kindly interested yourself, in order to render the last days of your aged brother a little more comfortable by enabling him to continue in a little usefulness to the end; not rusting, but wearing out.
>
> Wishing you every blessing of all short days and long days for a century to come.
>
> I am, dear Everett,
> Yours affectionately,
> Adam Clarke.[54]

Going back to the letter of Dr. Clarke, dated June 28, 1829, asking for missioners for the Shetland Isles, it would be hard for anyone to resist

---

[54] *Account*, Vol. 3, pp.264-7.

a compliment and enthusiasm like this. It indeed seems like Tabraham and others responded to these entreaties. But, less than a month before Adam Clarke's death, shocking news had come to him from the Shetlands. He explains how he first received the news in a letter he wrote, when in Bath, to Mrs. Tomkins on August 20, 1832:

> ....A few days ago my wife sent me an extract from a letter which had been sent me from Shetland, giving an account of a most calamitous event: a terrible storm at sea had fallen upon the poor fishing boats; about thirty boats, each containing five or six men, are supposed to have perished; many Methodists were in them and not a few leaders; the misery which has fallen to our lot is nearly forty widows and about two hundred orphans.[55]

A letter to Dr. Clarke from one of the Methodist missionaries, Robert Manwaring, supplied further details of the dreadful disaster in the Shetlands.

> Dear Doctor Clarke, It is my painful task to give you the most melancholy tidings that were ever sent you from Shetland. Monday, the 16th of August was a fine day which tempted the poor men who go to the Haaf, or fishing station, which is far from the shore; but about two o'clock on Tuesday morning, a tremendous gale arose from the west-by-north which blew until Saturday.... Some were seen to perish and we have still upwards of thirty boats away, of which we have heard nothing; among these are nine of our class leaders.... Lunnaness has suffered much, and there are, both in Whalsea and the Ness, many families left in a state of deep distress.... How many members we have lost in all I cannot tell, but we now have about forty widows and nearly 200 fatherless children belonging to our Society. Such scenes of wretchedness, such passionate distress, I have never before witnessed. Our own hearts have been rung with grief; in fact we are in the midst of widows and poor fatherless children. The poor, as I have told you, have been in the habit of helping the poor; now they are all, or nearly all, in the same circumstances.[56]

Dr. Clarke felt for the widows and orphans and he wrote hoping that not one landlord would attempt to take rent from such desperate people:

---

[55] *Account*, Vol. 3, pp.426-7.
[56] *Account*, Vol. 3, pp.427-9.

In such circumstances surely no landlord, even in the most barbarous countries, would attempt to exact the rent, of tenants who have lately perished in his service, from their widows and orphans. Whatever may be sent from this country, will be sent to relieve the present necessities of those most desolate persons, not to pay rents, &c.; as by the destruction of the lives of the men, all sources of gain are dried up and their widows and orphans left to the mercy of the public.... I hope that my friends, and the friends of God and the poor Shetlands, will come forward in the present distress, and such help as they are able to afford, and not suffer those most wretched of human beings utterly to perish.[57]

The news from the Shetlands was indeed devastating for Dr. Clarke. He had many times gone to the Shetlands and he was full of praise for its people and their devotion. He had spent long months in the area and the blow came finally when he was too ill to attend to it. In fifty years he had seen the ups and downs of Wesleyan Methodism but nothing of this sort had happened before. From his home at Haydon Hall, August 24, 1832, a week before Adam Clarke died, he wrote to a friend:

On my coming home on the 21st you may guess what I must have felt on receiving the following detail.... What to do I know not, nor where to turn: I have known no calamity in Shetland equal to this. Ireland is bad enough; but what is all their wretchedness, what is all their misery, compared to the present state of Shetland? I wrote to ---- about a school I wished to set up near B-----, a very desolate place; while we can we should work, and what we can we should perform. But what can I do for Shetland? Were it not so late in the year, I would set off thither.[58]

One month before his death he wrote the following testimonial and it is evident that he wished it to be permanent:

IN PERPETUAM REI MEMORIAM

I have lived more than threescore years and ten; I have travelled a good deal by land and sea; I have conversed with and seen many people, in and from many different countries; I have studied all the principal systems in the world; I have read much, thought much, and reasoned much. And the result is, I am persuaded of the simple, unadulterated truth of no book but the Bible; and of the excellence of no system of religion but that contained in the Holy Scriptures; and especially

---

[57] *Account*, Vol. 3, pp.429-30.
[58] *Account*, Vol. 3, p.433.

Christianity.... yet from a long and thorough knowledge of the subject, I am led most conscientiously to conclude that among Christianity itself as existing among those called Wesleyan Methodists is the purest, the safest and that which is most to the glory of God and the benefit of men.... And I believe that among them is to be found the best body of divinity that has ever existed in the church of Christ from its promulgation of Christianity to the present day. To him who would ask, 'Dr. Clarke, are you not a bigot?', without hesitation I would answer, 'No, I am not, for, by the grace of God, I am a Methodist.' Amen. Adam Clarke.[59]

Adam Clarke knew that his time was near. The constant travel and writing and preaching had wearied him and he sought to be near his family. He was a mighty man in prayer and when he led the daily worship in his family, they felt it to be the strong pleading of the friend of God. His mind went back to the poem he himself wrote in a lady's album:

I have enjoyed the spring of life;/ I have endured the toils of summer;/ I have culled the fruits of autumn;/ I am passing through the rigours of winter;/ And am neither forsaken by God/ Not [sic] abandoned by man./ I see at no great distance the dawn of a new day,/ The first of a spring that shall be eternal;/ It is advancing to meet me -/ I haste to embrace it:/ Welcome! Welcome! Eternal Spring! Hallelujah.[60]

The Conference that year (1832) was in Liverpool and Adam Clarke was chosen to preach the official Conference sermon and he was delighted to minister to the brethren. From Liverpool he went to Frome to visit his son, the Reverend Joseph Clarke. The public meeting in Frome was presided over by the Marquis of Bath and the Bishop of Bath and Wells and several other distinguished persons were present. Dr. Adam Clarke preached and the offering was large. The following Sunday he preached in the Wesleyan Chapel in Frome and then the following Sunday he preached at Westbury near Bristol. This was August 16, 1832 and his text was 1 Tim. 1:25, 'This is a faithful saying and worthy of all acceptation, that Jesus Christ came into the world to save sinners.' It was to be the final sermon. He

---

[59] Etheridge, pp.405-6.
[60] Maldwyn L. Edwards, *Adam Clarke* (London: Epworth Press, 1942), p.46; hereafter cited as 'Edwards'.

hurried home to Haydon Hall and the next day it was announced that he would preach in Bayswater and he arrived with Mr. and Mrs. Hobbs on the Saturday evening. On Sunday morning he was heard early in his room because he was an early riser. When Mr. Hobbs came downstairs, he was surprised to find Dr. Clarke fully dressed and ready to leave. He said: 'My dear fellow, you must get me home directly, without a miracle I could not preach; get me home, I want to be home.' [61] Mrs. Clarke was sent for but he was unable to speak to her. At eleven o'clock that night he entered upon Eternal Spring.

Dr. Clarke's death was announced in the *Wesleyan-Methodist Magazine* for September, 1832, in the following terms, with deep regret:

> We deeply regret to state, that intelligence has just reached us of the death of the Rev. Dr. Adam Clarke. He arrived at Bayswater, near London, at the house of Mr. Hobbs on Saturday, the 25th inst., intending to preach at the anniversary of the Methodist chapel in that place on the following morning. He was then in a state of ill-health, and became much worse early on Sunday morning, so as to be unable to fulfill his engagement. His disease, the malignant cholera, continued to increase, so as to baffle all the skill of physicians and the power of medicine; and he expired about twenty minutes past eleven o'clock on the evening of that day. He attended the late Conference in Liverpool, in his usual health and spirits, and preached twice with great energy and pathos during its sittings; he took also a lively interest in the business of the Conference, and the general affairs of the Connexion, and expressed the most cordial attachment to his brethren, and zeal for the furtherance of the cause of God. We stop the press to announce these particulars....[62]

Dr. Clarke was buried beside his one and only hero - John Wesley. This was in accordance with his oft-expressed wish, though in later years he had thoughts of being buried in Ireland. The interment took place on August 29, 1832, and the funeral was attended by members of his family and as many of the preachers who were able to attend. Henry Moore, his long-time friend and fellow countryman, was chosen to preach it and that sermon is recorded in full in the *Methodist Magazine* for the year 1832. Moore stated: 'Our Connexion, I believe,

---

[61] *Account*, Vol. 3, p.435.
[62] *Wesleyan-Methodist Magazine*, September, 1832, p.692.

never knew a more blameless life' than that of Dr. Clarke. He had his opponents; he had those who differ from him in doctrine, and sometimes in other things; but 'Not one even of his opponents could ever fix the least stain on his moral or religious character. Mr. Whitefield used to say, "A Preacher of the Gospel should be without spot." In the qualified sense.... in which.... the expression is to be taken, it certainly belonged to our deceased friend.'[63]

In the address of the British Conference to the Irish one in 1833, the statement reads: 'The venerable Dr. Clarke, through divine providence and grace, was a great gift from your country to ours, and to the general church of God, both now and in future ages.'[64] At the British Conference in Manchester there was an unseemly row concerning his obituary for the 1833 Minutes of Conference and several had to be written before the Conference was satisfied. Adam Clarke's critics would not permit any mention of his *Commentary* and his friends would not agree to any disparagement of his work. Eventually an obituary submitted by David McNichol was accepted, and in it there is no mention of the *Commentary* but the wording was to this effect:

> Without at all presuming that he was wholly free from defects, either as a man, a preacher, or a writer, we may yet safely place him in all these characters, among the great men of his age.... No man in any age of the Church was ever known for so long a period to have attracted larger audiences; no herald of salvation ever sounded forth his message with greater faithfulness or fervour – the fervour of love for Christ, and to the souls of perishing sinners; few ministers of the Gospel in modern times have been more honoured by the extraordinary unction of the Holy Spirit in their ministrations.[65]

Not long after Dr. Adam Clarke's passing a proposal was printed in the *Christian Advocate* to erect a monument to his memory. A committee was appointed for the purpose and many subscriptions were received. This project was never carried out because the Conference decided to have three memorials erected in Wesley's Chapel at City Road,

---

[63] *Wesleyan-Methodist Magazine*, October, 1832, p.724; and Gallagher, pp.98-9.
[64] Gallagher, p.99.
[65] Gallagher, pp.99-100.

London; one was to Joseph Benson, one to Richard Watson and one to Dr. Adam Clarke. The tribute to Adam Clarke reads as follows:

> In Memory of ADAM CLARKE, LL.D, F.S.A. Etc. A man of remarkable mental vigour, of almost unparalleled industry, and of extensive and varied learning. A Christian of deep and steadfast piety. Firmly attached to the essential doctrines and discipline of Wesleyan Methodism. A Preacher eminently evangelical, popular and useful for more than half a century. His praise is in all the churches. *Natus circiter* 1760: Obiit 1832.[66]

In the Methodist Church in Eastcote (now in north London, close to original site of Haydon Hall), there is also a memorial tablet to Dr. Adam Clarke which reads:

> To the Memory of ADAM CLARKE, M.A., LL.D. Born 1760 – Died 1832. A great Preacher. A profound Scholar. Theologian, Commentator, Author. Three times President of the Wesleyan Conference. Resided in Haydon Hall, Eastcote. 1824-1832. This Tablet was erected by the Trustees of Eastcote Chapel and friends of the Watford circuit.[67]

In the vestry of Eastcote Church there is an extract from the *Sunday Times* of September 2, 1832, recording the death of Dr. Adam Clarke, which reads:

> This eminent man ceased to live at a quarter past eleven on Sunday night. In 1805 his acquirements obtained the Honorary Degree of M.A., which was followed in 1806 by that of D.D., and subsequently by his election as a Member of the Royal Irish Academy. In late years he had lived in comparative retirement, but took a great interest in the progress of Christianity, especially in the Shetland Islands, where he was instrumental in establishing a Wesleyan Mission, which he continued to foster with great care. This venerable Divine was on Wednesday committed to the dust.[68]

---

[66] Gallagher, p.100.
[67] Gallagher, p.101.
[68] Gallagher, p.101.

In Ireland where he was born and lived for more than twenty years, two churches were erected as ADAM CLARKE memorials; one is in Portstewart, near Agherton, and built on the spot Dr. Clarke purchased for his eventide home, and the other on the spot in Portrush where Dr. Clarke opened his first

The 'New Church' in the parish of Agherton, near Portstewart, Co. Londonderry

Irish School on January 1, 1831. In front of the Church in Portrush there stands an obelisk, on one side of which is the inscription:

> In everlasting remembrance of Rev. Dr. Adam Clarke, *natus circiter* 1760, *obiit* 1832. A servant of the Most High, who in preaching the Gospel with great labours and apostolic grace for more than fifty years, showed to myriads the way of salvation, and by his Commentaries on the Holy Scriptures, and other works of piety and learning, yet speaks to passing generations. *Soli Gloria Deo.*

The other side carries the words:

> About the centenary of his birth, this obelisk, together with the Memorial Church at Portstewart, where he was brought up, has been erected by the subscriptions of the nobility, clergy, and the public at large of the British Islands, Canada and Australia, A.D. 1859. Look reader at this Memorial and learn that youth consecrated to God, unswerving integrity of life, zeal for the common good, and diligent improvement of mind and talent, can raise the obscure to renown and immortality.

The Commentator

Dr. Adam Clarke began to write his *Commentary* on May 1, 1798. He finished it on March 28, 1825, at eight o'clock in the evening, writing the remaining notes on the last chapter of Malachi upon his knees.

When it was done, he gave thanks to God, writing: 'To God the Father, Son and Holy Spirit, be eternal praise, Amen. I have this day completed this *Commentary*, on which I have laboured above thirty years; and which, when I began, I never expected to live long enough to finish. May it be a means of securing glory to God in the highest, to passing generations, and peace and good will among men upon earth! Amen, Amen.'[69] Later he speaks of the project of around twenty-eight years as one of delight and satisfaction.

> I may add that all these doctrines and all those connected with them, the incarnation and sacrificial death of Christ, his infinite, unoriginated, and eternal Deity, justification by faith in his blood, and the complete sanctification of the soul by the inspiration of the Holy Spirit, have not only been shown to be the doctrines of the sacred records, but have also been subjected to the strongest test of logical examination.... In this arduous labour I have had no assistants, not ever a single week's help from an amanuensis; no person to look for common-places, or refer to an ancient author; to find out the place and transcribe a passage of Greek or Latin, or any other language to verify a quotation.... I have laboured alone for nearly twenty-five years previously to the work being sent to the press.[70]

We have the family memorandum that on that evening when the work was finished, Dr. Clarke came into the parlour and without speaking, told his youngest son to come into the study. On entering he found the usual signs of work all laid aside, the books marshalled in their shelves, the study table clear and all but the Bible cleared away. The Doctor then spoke:

> This, Joseph, is the happiest period I have enjoyed for years: I have put the last hand to my Comment. I have written the last word. I have put away the chains that would remind me of my bondage; and there.... have I returned the deep thanks of a grateful soul to the God who has shown me such great and continued kindness. I shall now go into the parlour, tell my good news to the rest, and enjoy myself for the day.[71]

---

[69] Adam Clarke, *Commentary and Critical Notes,* Haydon Hall, Middlesex, Monday, March 28, 1825; hereafter cited as 'Clarke, *Commentary*', see also 'Abbreviations' for bibliographical notes.

[70] Clarke, *Commentary*, p. 3478, Eastcott, April 17, 1826.

[71] Etheridge, p.325.

The whole *Commentary* is replete with quotations and it is a thesaurus of languages and dialects. All sixty-six books are referred to with ample illustrations and there is a large section of Hebrew, Greek and Latin quotations. All this is the work of one man and out of the twenty-eight years he has given for production, and twenty years and more of moving at regular intervals. Adam Clarke had worked as an itinerant minister in Bradford, Norwich, St. Austell, Plymouth, the Norman Isles, Bristol, Dublin, Manchester, Liverpool, London, Bristol (the second time), Liverpool (the second time), Manchester (the second time) and now in London. He had worked in fourteen circuits altogether and it was during his tenth circuit that he developed his love for commenting on the scriptures. For a period of ten years, 1810 to 1819, he had been a servant of state and altogether his work on the *Commentary* was interrupted by one programme after another. For ten years his time was taken up with the *Foedera* and the *Commentary*, but his time was also taken up with uninterrupted ministerial duty and preaching.

When the first volume appeared, 'Genesis to Deuteronomy', Dr. Clarke was sharply criticized for his suggestion that the animal in Genesis 3 was a baboon. In Genesis 3:1, 2, 4, 13, 14, Clarke translated the word *nachash* as baboon and although he was the only one that chose it; he was not repentant.

> If any person should choose to differ from the opinion stated above, he is at perfect liberty so to do; I make it no article of faith, nor of Christian communion; I crave the same liberty to judge for myself that I give to others, to which every man has an indisputable right; and I hope no man will call me a heretic for departing in this respect from the common cause opinion, which appears to me so embarrassed as to be altogether unintelligible.[72]

In the *General Preface* to his work, Dr. Clarke speaks approvingly of the commentaries he has used in preparing for his notes, and among them he has listed Augustine (354-430), Hugo Grotius (1583-1645), John Calvin (1509-1564), Matthew Poole (1624-1679), John Lightfoot (1602-1675), Simon Patrick (1626-1707), Matthew Henry (1662-1714), John Gill (1697-1771), Phillip Doddridge (1702-1751), John

---

[72] Clarke, *Commentary*: notes on Genesis Ch. 3, v.1, in. loco.

Wesley (1703-1791), Thomas Coke (1747-1814), and a host of others; but Clarke is the only one who selects *nachash* to represent a baboon. No sooner had Dr. Clarke published his notes on Genesis than an army of critics descended on the baboon passage, and they began to make banter of this passage. In one of the public papers these lines appeared:

LINES ON THE NACHASH
The Rev. Dr. Adam Clarke asserts
It could not be a serpent tempted Eve,
But a gay monkey whose mimic arts
And fopperies were most likely to deceive.
Dogmatic commentators still hold out
A *serpent*, not a *monkey*, tempted Madam;
And which shall we believe? without a doubt
None knows so well what tempted EVE, as ADAM.[73]

Readers who looked forward to Clarke's *Commentaries* being published, were highly embarrassed to see the fun made of a highly important passage like Genesis 3. Not one of the illustrious commentators argued this, and no one since Clarke has made use of it. The rest of Genesis was overlooked, and wherever Dr. Clarke was ready to preach, Genesis 3 was brought up. The critics of Dr. Clarke were adamant that in his obituary in the 1833 Methodist Conference, no mention should be made of Clarke's *Commentaries*. Neither was it mentioned in the Irish Methodist Conference with regard to Dr. Clarke, nor was it mentioned in the Wesley's Chapel memorial, nor was it mentioned in the Eastcoat Methodist Church memorial (except the word 'Commentator' is used), nor was it in the Portrush obelisk, except the comment, 'Commentaries on Holy Scriptures.' All of these memorials make no mention that he was credited with being the author of the commentary on Genesis.

All this argument obscures the fact that there are many fine passages in the book of Genesis and chapter twenty-two, verse 8, is a typical one.

Verse 8. *My son, God will provide himself a lamb.* Here we find the same obedient unshaken faith for which this pattern of practical piety was ever remarkable. But we must not suppose that this was the

---

[73] Quoted in: Edwards, p.33.

language merely of faith and obedience; the patriarch spoke prophetically and referred to that Lamb of God which HE had provided for himself, who in the fullness of time should take away the sin of the world, and of whom Isaac was a most expressive type. All the other lambs which had been offered.... had been such as men *chose* and men *offered*; but THIS was the Lamb which GOD had provided – emphatically, THE Lamb of God.[74]

In the New Testament, Dr. Clarke was questioned about his comments on Judas Iscariot, whom Clarke thought did betray Jesus. In all of these Judas Iscariot passages: Matt. 10:4, 26:14, 26:25, 26:47, 27:3; Mark 3:19, 14:10, 14:43; Luke 6:16, 22:3, 22:47, 22:48; John 6:71, 12:4, 13:2, 13:26, 13:29, 18:2, 18:3, 18:5; and Acts 1:16, 1:25, Dr. Clarke presents Judas with an awful crime, and in an addendum to Acts, chapter one, he writes on Judas in more detail.

> The utmost that can be said for the case of Judas is this: he committed a heinous act of sin and ingratitude; but he repented and did what he could to undo his wicked act.... I contend that the chief priests, &c., who instigated Judas to deliver up his Master.... were *worse* men than Judas Iscariot himself; and that, if mercy was extended to those, the wretched penitent traitor did not die out of the reach of the yearning of its bowels. And I contend, farther, that there is no positive evidence of the final damnation of Judas in the sacred text.[75]

In spite of all that, Dr. Clarke argues it is very difficult to get round Acts 1:25. When Judas is dead, the church met to appoint another in Judas's place. Two men were appointed to take Judas's place and then they prayed. 'Thou, Lord, which knowest the hearts of all men.... which Judas by transgression fell, that he might go to his own place.' This is serious and important language. By saying with the Scriptures that Judas has gone 'where he belongs', no man or woman should say that the Scriptures were silent on the fate of the wicked. John Wesley has the comment: '*To go to his own place* - That which his crimes had deserved, and which he had chosen for himself, far from the other apostles, in the region of death.'[76] While commenting on Mark 14:21, Dr. Clarke is silent over the doom presented by Jesus. 'Woe to that

---

[74] Clarke, *Commentary*: note on *Genesis*, Ch. 22, v.8.
[75] Clarke, *Commentary*: note in Addendum to Acts 1.
[76] John Wesley, *Explanatory Notes upon The New Testament*, note on Acts 1:25.

man by whom the Son of man is betrayed; good were it for that man if he had never been born.' It deals with Judas and his transgression act, but Dr. Clarke is silent. While Clarke is content to say, 'There is no positive evidence of the final damnation of Judas in the sacred text', he misses the point when Jesus says, '….for that man if he had never been born.' Four times Jesus utters these solemn words on Judas Iscariot: Matt. 26:24, 25; Mark 14:21; Luke 22:21, 22; John 13:26, 27. Dr. Clarke would have been wiser to deal with the texts as they appear and not to have given the impression that there is no evidence in the text that Judas stands condemned.

Before Adam Clarke went to Bradford, Wiltshire, in 1782, he had drawn up a document which represented his creed in thirty-two propositions. Only one item is out of tune with the rest of the thirty-one, and that is Proposition Ten. On his doctrine of the human and divine nature, he comments:

> His *Human Nature*,…. because God, infinite and eternal, is uncreated, underived, and unbegotten; and which, were it otherwise, He could not be *God* in any proper sense of the word: but He is most explicitly declared to be God in the Holy Scriptures; and therefore the doctrine of the Eternal Sonship must necessarily by false.[77]

Clarke was adamant that the doctrine of the Divine Sonship of the Redeemer was not scriptural and he held this position all his life. When the question was discussed, it was not discussed in vain. It was not done in a tribal way but added to the revelation that the Divine Sonship of the Redeemer was in fact eternal and therefore all Christians held to the doctrine of the Saviour of the world. We must go to the Scriptures with a humble and believing will, and it is there that not only in the Divine Subsistence there are three Persons, but that the relationship of the Second Person to the first is that of Son. Adam Clarke was a serious believer in the Trinity but he hesitated on this relationship. He became clear that the name 'the Son of God' was a Messianic title of the Redeemer as the consequence of his having been born of a virgin, but he denied that it was descriptive of His mode of existence prior to the Incarnation.

---

[77] *Account*, Vol. 1, p.173.

Divine revelation affirms that the only-begotten Son was in the Father and that God so loved this world He was willing to give His only Son, and God sent him to this world and He was born of Mary. We know in the deep mysteries of God, who made all flesh, that the glory He displayed was the glory of the only-begotten of the Father. Of course Adam Clarke believed this and taught it, but not as the eternally begotten of the Father because, on his view, there was no relationship. On these groups Adam Clarke made a divergence from the faith of the catholic church. We see from Scripture that the church from the beginning had taken these emphatic statements and taught that the Second Person of the Trinity is by an ineffable and eternal generation the Son of God. The Creeds also confirmed on this matter. Even before the increasing heresy of the fourth century had necessitated the church to affirm this doctrine at the first council of Nicaea (AD 325), most of the great Christian communities had accepted this particular doctrine as a profession of faith.

At Antioch, where the disciples were first called Christians this point was made: 'I believe in one Lord Jesus Christ, His only begotten Son, born of Him before the world; True God of True God, by whom also the worlds were framed, and all things made.' At Jerusalem, in the Catechetical Lectures of St. Cyril (bishop there in AD 345), is found: 'I believe in one Lord Jesus Christ, the only-begotten Son of God, begotten of the Father before all ages; the true God, by whom all things were made.' In Nicaea the universal Church pronounced the faith once delivered to the saints, and called upon the faithful in all ages to abide by the same truth: 'We believe in one Lord Jesus Christ, the Son of God, the only-begotten of the Father; that is, of the substance of the Father, God of God, Light of Light, very God of very God; begotten, not made; consubstantial with the Father; by whom all things were made.'[78]

Adam Clarke had a great abhorrence of Arianism, yet with this main point in the testimony of the Church against Arianism he still could not bring his mind to concur. He had embraced, and for ever held, certain arguments which prevented him from believing that 'the Son of

---

[78] Etheridge, pp.329-330.

God was begotten of the Father before all worlds.' About 1787, Adam Clarke had written out his Creed against the Eternal Sonship, and in a letter to Mr. Wesley he took the liberty to read it to him. John Wesley wrote that in holding this doctrine against the Eternal Sonship, he was in danger of departing from the true faith of the Church. Adam felt for Wesley his unbounded admiration and when John Wesley died on the March 2, 1791, he was overwhelmed with grief, but being in Dublin it was too far away to go to the funeral. Adam felt the blow personally but he never changed his Article Ten, despite John Wesley's pleas.

Adam Clarke was still surprised that so many men in Conference held his holding of this doctrine as an *animus* against him and used it as a sort of ecclesiastical persecution. The question has now been long decided and settled, and most of the pamphlets which carried and debated the question are now out of print. Richard Watson in his *Remarks on the Eternal Sonship of Christ* (London, January 10, 1818), wrote an answer to Adam Clarke. Watson stated clearly that he had no feelings but respect towards Dr. Clarke and a high sense of his talents and virtue. Nevertheless, Watson was adamant that Clarke opposed Arian and Socinian rules of interpreting Scripture and said, 'I strongly protest against this being construed into an insinuation that I associate Dr. Clarke with the theologians of either class.' In eighty-four pages, Richard Watson defends his interpretation of the doctrine of eternal Sonship.

> This subject is in itself of the highest importance connected as it is with the personality of our Lord. If there be not a Trinity of Persons in the Godhead, I cannot conceive of a divine atonement for sins. If God had not a Son to send into the world, by whom the world might be saved, no other being in heaven or earth was adequate to offer a full, perfect, and sufficient oblation and satisfaction for the sins of the human race.... Besides "Son of God", there is, as far as I recollect, no other term applied to Christ, which simply, and in itself, and without recurring to other evidence, expresses his divine personality. "Lord" does not;.... "Jesus" does not;.... "Christ" does not;.... "Word" does not.... But let the term "Son of God" be established as the scriptural designation of the divine nature of our Lord and Saviour, and the idea of divine and proper personality is eternally preserved in our opinions respecting him: Let us show, first, that the Son is divine, and we escape Socinianism; and, second, that he is divine as a Son, and we shun the Sabellian heresy; -

that sliding path which infallibly, though by easy descent, has conducted thousands to join the rank of those who "deny the Lord that bought them."[79]

Richard Treffry (Junior, 1804-1838) in his book *Inquiry into the Doctrine of the Eternal Sonship of our Lord Jesus Christ,* has answered Clarke sufficiently. Treffry's work has taken its place among English theological classics, and Adam Clarke, while he lived, was ever grateful because Treffry hailed him with boundless admiration. The book is replete with quotations and illustrations from Scripture, as well as those of the Church Fathers of the first five centuries.[80] Treffry makes mention of Dr. Clarke's writings in his pages and it is no less than generous because he does it with warm counsel.

Treffry draws attention to John 5:5-18, where John makes Christ to say that he calls God his Father, making him say that God and he were equal:

> [He represented Himself].... as the Son of God.... and [this] was the occasion of the exacerbation there manifested.... This breach of the law, as by His enemies it was represented, afforded a suitable pretext for attempting His life. Our Redeemer offered no apology for His conduct. He preferred affirming His Divine and paramount authority: "My Father worketh hitherto, and I work" [v.17]. The result is worthy of especial attention. "Therefore the Jews sought the more to kill Him, because He not only had broken the Sabbath, but said also that God was His proper Father,.... making himself equal with God." [v. 18]. Here the calling of God *His own Father* was understood by the Jews, and their opinion is sanctioned by the Evangelist, as a most direct and precise claim to Divinity, and, according to their interpretation, as a crime worthy of death.[81]

On Hebrews 3:1-6, Treffry draws an argument from Christ being superior to Moses:

---

[79] Richard Watson, 'Remarks on the Eternal Sonship of Christ', in: *The Works of The Rev. Richard Watson*, (12 vols. London: John Mason, 1834-1837), Vol. 7, pp.84-5; hereafter cited as 'Watson, *Works*'.

[80] Etheridge, p.331.

[81] Richard Treffry, Jun., *An Enquiry into the Doctrine of the Eternal Sonship of our Lord Jesus Christ* (4th Edition; London: Wesleyan Conference Office, 1865), pp.89-90; hereafter cited as 'Treffry'.

Accordingly he [he writer of Hebrews] argues, "Jesus - was worthy of more glory than Moses, inasmuch as the builder hath more honour than the house" (v. 3). The founder of a household or family, he who frames its regulations, arranges its grades of dignity or service, and maintains its order, has more honour than the entire household.... The principle here involved, the apostle goes on to suggest, is one universally recognised. Every house is.... [built], every family is founded, every household is arranged and established by some one; and in all such cases we see the same law of distinction and pre-eminence. But in the example before us there is one sublime peculiarity. He that built all things, that constructed the vast universe,.... is the Son [and], He is God. That fact, therefore, by which our Lord is distinguished from Moses, that which, according to the common reason of mankind, constitutes His perfect and unapproachable glory, plainly is, that He is – God.... Moses, indeed, as the servant, was faithful *in* the household, of which he was himself a part;.... but Christ, as the Son, who framed all things, established the household, and is the true God, is *over* His house in absolute lordship and sovereignty.[82]

Maintaining that the work of redemption is put in jeopardy by arguing that Jesus is less than God, Treffry goes on to argue for a full recognition of Jesus the Christ:

The Son of God has borne our nature up to heaven, and placed it "on the right hand of the Majesty on high, far above all principality, and power, and might, and dominion, and every name which is named, not only in this world, but also in that which is to come" (Eph. 1, 21). And as the souls of His people have been transformed into the image of His Divine and eternal nature, as they have thus become the sons of God, so in due time their bodies also, redeemed from the power of the grace, shall be modelled after His glorious body: they shall "bear the image of the heavenly;"..... The Father loveth the Son. The Father judgeth no man, but hath committed all judgment unto the Son; that all men should honour the Son, even as they honour the Father. He that honoureth not the Son honoureth not the Father that hath sent Him.... Unbelief dishonours the Son of God; and high as is His dignity, so deep is the turpitude of the sin.... Unbelief dishonours the love of God in the gift of the Son, and the development of the Divine purity in the death of the

---

82   Treffry, pp.292-3.

Son. It does despite to the entire system of evangelical truth, and converts the choicest balm into the fellest [most lethal] poison.[83]

Treffry closes his *Inquiry* with a section on the ancient creeds. Up until the fifth century, they were supposed to state the case wherein all Christians spoke the same language but there were minor differences. Treffry picks out the Nicene Creed and publicizes that for which the Council had been convened in 325AD:

….As to its substance, the fathers were of the same mind; but, in respect to the sovereign Deity of Christ, they judged it inadequate to the evasions of the Arians. They increased its precision, therefore, adding especially the express assertion of the consubstantiality of the Son with the Father…. In this latter term, differing but in one letter from that which the Arians allowed, the Nicene fathers found the only test of Arianism, and the only security against its gigantic errors…. At the conclusion of the creeds, however, the variation is considerable; for while that of Caesarea gives a general affirmation of the…. doctrine of the Trinity, the Nicene, as having especially to do with the person of the Son, affixes an anathema to the particular errors for the suppression of which it was designed…. [The Nicene creed says:] "But those who say that there was a time when the Son of God was not, and that He was not before He was born, or that He was made from nothing, or of any other essence or substance, or created, or subject to alteration or change, such persons the catholic and apostolic church anathematizes."…. On this ground the fathers, when they had affirmed the Son to be *homoousios*, immediately subjoined, that the catholic church anathematizes such as say that He was created, &c.; so that it might be understood that He who confessed the Son to be *homoousios*, did, in fact, truly and sincerely declare Him to be the Son of God, according to the right import of that Scripture, "I and My Father are one;" and, "He that seeth Me seeth My Father also." The Nicene creed was designed as a standard of doctrine upon the person of Christ.[84]

Treffry concludes his argument by looking carefully at all the creeds of the Church and finishes by looking at the Athanasian Creed:

Next to the Niceno-Constantinopolitan, the creed which goes under the name of St. Athanasius has most widely obtained; and this is the more remarkable since it neither originated in, nor was confirmed by, a

---

83 Treffry, pp.380-2.
84 Treffry, pp.454-458.

General Council. Without entering into the controversies to which this composition has given rise.... it is probably of Latin origin, and belongs to the latter end of the fourth or the beginning of the fifth century. The following versicles are appropriate to our subject:- "The Father is made of none; neither created nor begotten. / The Son is of the Father alone: not made, not created but begotten. / Our Lord Jesus Christ, the Son of God, is God and man....".

There is a contemporary relic of antiquity to which it would be unjust not to refer. I allude to the *Te Deum*. Nothing can be more clear than its affirmation of our Lord's eternal Sonship, and of the catholicity of the doctrine. "The holy Church throughout all the world doth acknowledge Thee. The Father of an infinite Majesty; Thine honourable, true and only Son; Also the Holy Ghost, the Comforter. Thou art the King of Glory, O Christ; Thou are the everlasting.... Son of the Father....".

This magnificent composition has now, for sixteen hundred years, been employed by the Christian church; and Sabbath after Sabbath,.... thousands of devout worshippers, in harmony with "the holy church throughout all the world," have adored the first Person of the Trinity as "the Father of an infinite Majesty;" and the second Person of the Trinity as "the eternal Son of the Father."[85]

Treffry concludes his historic essay by giving an assessment:

The reader has now before him a body of evidence sufficient, it is presumed, to prove the antiquity of any doctrine. As far as our means of information extend, we find that the eternal Sonship of our Lord has been held by the Christian church from the time of the apostles. Not only was it to be believed, and was actually believed, by the primitive ministers and doctors, but by every recognised professor of Christianity. From a very early period, its avowal, in terms the most express, emphatical, and unambiguous, was demanded of every candidate for Christian baptism, and none who refused such an avowal could be admitted to that rite.[86]

Before we leave this argument concerning Dr. Adam Clarke and his refusal to withdraw his allegations about the eternal Sonship of our Lord, there are two books that will bear directly upon the occasion. Both are written (anonymously) by John Middleton Hare; the first is

---

[85] Treffry, pp.462- 463.
[86] Treffry, p.463.

entitled, *The Life and Labours of Adam Clarke, LL.D.: To which is added An Historical Sketch of the controversy concerning the Sonship of Christ*, London, 1834. The second is entitled, *The Life and Labours of Adam Clarke, LL.D.*,[87] printed in London and the date is 1842. The second edition drops the sub-title and the *Historical Sketch*, for reasons explained in the Preface: 'The narrative has been divested of the somewhat controversial aspect which in several parts it bore; and it now contains nothing that needs give offence to the most sensitive partizan of any class of opinions.'[88] J.M. Hare was the eldest son of Edward Hare (1773-1818), and the father of twelve children and a journalist, essayist and poet. The leading Wesleyan Methodists wanted to play down the eternal Sonship of Christ controversy, and it is really remarkable that a book first printed in 1834 and dealing in detail with the controversy, then makes no mentioned of it by 1842. Of course the controversy just didn't go away but the Wesleyan Methodists clearly wanted it covered up.

John Middleton Hare firmly supported Clarke in the *Controversy*, and blamed Christians in the first few centuries with propagating 'the Eternal Sonship theory' on the Church.

> In consequence of the Christian Fathers adopting these philosophising tenets, and mixing them up with the Gospel of Jesus Christ, their writings were soon filled with notions of celestial generations and productions in almost endless succession. Here we have the origin of the Eternal Sonship theory in the Christian church. What was taught of the generations and productions of *aenons* [sic] by the oriental philosophers, was retained by these accommodating Christian Fathers, under the character of Eternal Sonship, and taught as the divine generation of the Son of God. They applied to the Godhead, exclusively, the terms which are applied to Christ in his incarnate state *only*; and thus established what they denominate his eternal generation.... But it is singular fact,

---

[87] [John Middleton Hare], *The Life and Labours of Adam Clarke, LL.D., to which is added An Historical Sketch of the Controversy Concerning the Sonship of Christ, particularly as connected with the proceedings of the Wesleyan Methodist Conference* (London: John Stephens, 1834), hereafter cited as 'Hare, 1834'; and [John Middleton Hare], *The Life and Labours of Adam Clarke, LL.D.* (Second Edition. London: Longman, Brown, Green, and Longmans, 1842), hereafter cited as 'Hare, 1842'.

[88] Hare, 1842, p.iii.

that the doctrine of an inferior Deity, owing his existence to another, a doctrine against which St. John wrote his gospel, and which Justin denounces as blasphemy, became, in about forty years from the time when the latter wrote, the orthodoxy of the day.[89]

This doctrine of the Eternal Sonship of Jesus is traced by Hare through the gospels and epistles and further with proofs from the Fathers. Hare appears to have no difficulty in including John Wesley in that number.

> The doctrine of God producing the divine nature of Christ out of his own substance, is now generally discarded, as incompatible with the supreme Godhead of Christ, which is so clearly taught in the Scriptures; and the filial relation is considered as belonging to his complex character, as God and man united in one person.... It cannot be successfully denied, that the writings of Wesley, Coke, Drew, Benson, Robinson, and Dr. Adam Clarke, upon the divinity of Christ, have been so extensively read by this community, that they are incapable of receiving the semi-Arianism of the late Richard Watson, or that of the editor of the *Wesleyan-Methodist Magazine*. A controversy, however, has existed in the Wesleyan-Methodist Connexion for some years; and some of the leading men in the Conference, have laboured hard to establish the doctrine of what is called the eternal generation, or Sonship, of Christ, as a doctrine of the Holy Scriptures.[90]

Hare then introduces Adam Clarke, maintaining that he has written 'a simple argument in his Note on Luke 1:35, which argument is absolutely unanswerable.' Clearly Mr. Hare knows where he stands! Various attempts have been made to persuade Clarke to refute the note he wrote, but Dr. Adam Clarke has gone to his grave without writing a refusal. Richard Watson was the person that Hare did not like as a theologian and he gives short shrift to his doctrine.

> Mr. Richard Watson wrote repeatedly in defence of this false doctrine. He is allowed to be the ablest advocate that it has had in modern days; and to this honour he is justly entitled. His writings have not, however, always produced conviction, because they are sometimes at variance with themselves, as well as with the Holy Scriptures.... This controversy is of an unhappy character. No one can read what Mr. Watson has written upon this subject, and not feel sensibly that a gigantic mind has

---

[89] Hare, 1834, pp.449- 450. Note: the word '*aenons*' appears to be a typographical error in Hare's text, and probably should read as 'aeons'.

[90] Hare, 1834, pp.462-463.

put forth all its energies, to prove a blasphemous doctrine; and no one can read the Replies of Mr. Exley, and others, without feeling as deeply that Mr. Watson has attributed to Dr. Clarke, opinions which he never held; that every argument which he uses is a glaring sophism; and that every passage which he adduces in support of his views, is flagrantly perverted. No one can wonder why he quarrels with the Doctor for recommending the exercise of reason and understanding in reading the Scriptures.[91]

If John Middleton Hare should write, in 1834, so firmly asserting his denial of the Eternal Sonship of Christ – why would he publish another volume just eight years later and leave out the *Controversy*? In that short space of time he evidently felt that Wesleyan Methodists could read a volume on the life and character of Dr. Clarke, but that to continue the *Controversy* would serve no good purpose.

Dr. Adam Clarke was sound and scriptural in his theology. No one has shown that he, by his life and work, has failed to maintain that great truth that Jesus Christ, his Saviour, was 'over all, God blessed for ever'; and Clarke made this truth known by preaching it, writing it, and living and dying in the same blessed truth. In his public preaching he carefully abstained from making an illustration touching on the 'controversy'; and when President of the Methodist Conference, he was studiously exact in obtaining from each candidate a statement on the Lord Jesus Christ consistent with the agreed theology of his brethren.

Dr. Adam Clarke's *Commentary* on the Bible is rich and satisfying. Of course, with its author, alone, doing all sixty-six books of the Bible, it is not equal in all its parts. On the Pentateuch and the Gospels, there is good work. Dr. Clarke is not a slave to anyone and it is quite certain that it took him nearly thirty years to have it all done, and for about twenty-two years he was labouring elsewhere. He had gone over the kingdom of Great Britain many times and for ten years he was in control over the *Foedera* papers. On the Apostolic Epistles he is fine, on the historical books he is satisfactory, but on the prophetic books he is wanting. Almost two hundred years have gone by since the *Commentary* was published - and yet it was by one man alone, so his

---

[91] Hare, 1834, pp.472-3 and pp.481-482.

fame is certain. On both sides of the Atlantic, Adam Clarke's fame still lives on; and even today readers can find some of the satisfaction from the use of his *Commentary* that Clarke's biographer, Dr. John Wesley Etheridge (1804-1866), clearly did.

> Its luminous expositions of the Law and the Gospel;.... its earnest and forcible appeals to the conscience of the sinner and unbeliever; its rich counsels for the well-understood wants of the Christian's inner life; its endless exhibitions of general knowledge, and its valuable aids to the students of those holy tongues in which revelation took its first recorded forms; - all will render this book the companion and the counsellor of multitudes as long as the English language may endure.[92]

Adam Clarke, on the Second Coming of our Lord, when he comments on our Lord's appearing, deals with the passage in 1 Thessalonians 4:13-17, and puts the Lord's people in wonder and glory as he deals with it. It is the first letter that Paul wrote, and he deals with eternal glory and the hope of His coming. Beginning with chapter four, verse 13, he encourages them to look up and see what is gone before. '*I would not that you be ignorant.*' This was the point *lacking in their faith* that Paul intended to instruct them; Clarke comments thus:

> [*Them which are asleep*] That is, those who are *dead*.... To set them right on this important subject, he delivers three important truths: 1. He asserts, as he has done before, that they who died in the Lord should have, in virtue of Christ's resurrection, a resurrection unto eternal life and blessedness. 2. He makes a new discovery, that the *last generation* should not die at all, but be in a moment changed to immortals. 3. He adds another new discovery, that, though the living should not die, but be transformed, yet the dead should first be raised, and be made glorious and immortal; and so, in some measure, have the preference and advantage of such as shall then be found alive.[93]

Those who are alive and see what is happening should not be afraid, for then they see themselves raptured and taken up:

> [*We which are alive, and remain*] By the pronoun *we* the apostle does not intend *himself*, and the *Thessalonians* to whom he was writing; he is speaking of the genuine Christians which shall be found on earth when

---

[92] Etheridge, p.333.

[93] Adam Clarke, *The Holy Bible.... Commentary and Critical Notes....*, (8 vols, London: 1810-1824; and later editions; hereafter cited as 'Clarke, *Commentary*'), 1 Thess. 4:13.

56

Christ comes to judgment.... [*Shall not prevent them which are asleep*] Those who shall be found living in that day, though they shall not pass through death, but be suddenly changed, shall not go to glory *before* them that are dead, *for the dead in Christ shall rise first* – they shall be raised, their bodies made glorious, and be caught up to meet the Lord, *before* the others shall be changed.... Those who shall be found alive on that day shall not anticipate glory before the dead in Christ; for they shall rise *first*, and begin the enjoyment of it before the others shall be changed.[94]

Then Clarke comments on how the glorious event shall happen!:

[*The Lord himself*] That is: Jesus Christ *shall descend from heaven*; shall descend in like manner as he was seen by his disciples to ascend, i.e. in his human form, but now infinitely more glorious.... Observe the order of this terribly glorious day: 1. Jesus, in all the dignity and splendour of his eternal Majesty, *shall descend from heaven*.... 2. Then the.... shout.... shall be given for the dead to arise. 3. Next the archangel, as the *herald* of Christ, shall repeat the order.... 4. When all the dead in Christ are raised, then the *trumpet shall sound,* as the signal for them all to flock together to the throne of Christ.... 5. When the dead in Christ are raised, their vile bodies being made like unto his glorious body, then, 6. Those who are *alive* shall be *changed*, and made immortal. 7. These shall be *caught up together with them to meet the Lord in the air.* .... What an inexpressibly terrific glory will then be exhibited![95]

In the second epistle to the Thessalonians, Paul deals with those to whom the darkness of death is reserved for ever. This is dealt with first in chapters one, verses 8 to 9. The rapture is past and now Clarke's comment turns to those who have rejected Christ:

[*In flaming fire*].... - inflicting just punishment *on them that know not God;* the heathen who do not worship the true God.... the *Jews,* particularly who have rejected the gospel.... and all nominal Christians who, though they believe the gospel as a revelation from God, yet do not obey it as a rule of life.... [*Who shall be punished*] What this *everlasting destruction* consists in we cannot tell.... for a part of this punishment consists in being banished from the *presence of the Lord* – excluded from his *approbation* for ever.... [*The glory of his power*]

94 Clarke, *Commentary*, 1 Thess. 4:15.
95 Clarke, *Commentary*, 1 Thess. 4:16.

Never to see the face of God throughout eternity is a heart-rending, soul-appalling thought; and to *banished* from the *glory of his power*, that power the *glory* of which is peculiarly manifested in *saving the lost* and *glorying the faithful*, is what cannot be reflected on without confusion and dismay. But this must be the lot of all *who acknowledge not God, and obey not the gospel of our Lord Jesus Christ*. Verse 10. [*When he shall come to be glorified in his saints*] As the grace of God is peculiarly glorified in saving sinners and making them into *saints*, this gracious *power* will be particularly manifested in the great day, when countless millions will appear before that throne who have come out of great tribulation, who have washed their robes and made them white in the blood of the Lamb.[96]

In closing this chapter, Dr. Adam Clarke points to the destruction of the wicked who will not flee to the Lord Jesus who is able to save:

The *everlasting destruction* of the ungodly is a subject that should be continually placed before the eyes of men by the preachers of the Gospel. How shall a man be induced to take measures to escape a danger of the existence of which he is not convinced? Show him the *hell* which the justice of God has lighted up for the devil and his angels; and in which all Satan's children and followers must have their eternal portion.... *everlasting destruction* from the presence of the Lord and the glory of his power. And if God did not award this to such persons, he could not be the *God of justice*.... Another proof of the fall and degeneracy of men is, their general enmity to the *doctrine of holiness*; they cannot bear the thought of being sanctified through body, soul, and spirit, so as to perfect holiness in the fear of God. A spurious kind of Christianity is gaining ground in the world. Weakness, doubtfulness, littleness of faith, consciousness of inward corruptions, and sinful infirmities of different kinds, are by some considered the highest proofs of a *gracious state*; whereas in the primitive Church they would have been considered as evidences that the persons in question had received just light enough to show them their wretchedness and danger, but not the healing virtue of the blood of Christ.[97]

In 1 Timothy 2:4-6, Dr. Clarke points out that as Jesus Christ is Lord and God, the finality of the death of Christ should be the symphony on

---

[96] Clarke, *Commentary*, 2 Thess. 1:8-10.
[97] Clarke, *Commentary*, end of chapter, 2 Thess. 1.

which all should be agreed. Christ Jesus died that all may come to him and there is no excuse why preachers should be divided.

Verse 4. [*Who will have all men to be saved*] Because he wills the salvation of all men; therefore, he wills that all men should be prayed for. In the face of such a declaration, how can any Christian soul suppose that God ever unconditionally and eternally reprobated any man? Those who can believe so, one would suppose, can have little acquaintance either with the *nature* of God, or the *bowels of Christ*. [*And to come unto the knowledge of the truth*] The truth – the gospel of Christ, should be *proclaimed* to them; and it is the duty of all who know it, to diffuse it far and wide; and when it is made known, then it is the duty of those who hear it to acknowledge and receive it…. Verse 5. …. [*And one mediator*]…. God was offended with the crimes of men; to restore them to his peace, Jesus Christ was incarnated; and being God and man…. both God and men met in and were reconciled by him. Verse 6. [*Who gave himself a ransom*]…. As God is the God and Father of all,…. and Jesus Christ the mediator of all, so he gave his life a ransom for all…. As surely as God has created all men, so surely has Christ Jesus died for all men.[98]

As Dr. Clarke gets to the end of his *Commentary*, he has a word with all his readers:

Verse 17. …. [*And whosoever will*] No soul is excluded: Jesus died for every man; every man may be saved; therefore let him who *wills*, who *wishes* for salvation, come and take the water *of life freely* – without money or price! Verse 18. [*If any man shall add*] Shall give any other meaning to these prophecies, or any other application of them, than God intends, *he*, though not originally intended, shall have the plagues threatened in this book for his portion. Verse 19. [*If any man shall take away*] If any man shall lessen this meaning, curtail the sense, explain away the spirit and design, of these prophecies, *God shall take away his part out of the book of life, &c.* Thus Jesus warns all those who consider this book to beware of indulging their own conjectures concerning it. I confess that this warning has its own powerful influence upon my mind, and has prevented me from indulging my own conjectures concerning its meaning, or of adopting the conjectures of others. These visions and threatenings are too delicate and awful a subject to trifle with, or even to treat in the most solemn manner, where the meaning is obscure. I must leave these things to *time* and *event*, the surest interpreters. No jot or

---

[98] Clarke, *Commentary*, 1 Timothy 2:4-6.

tittle of Christ's word shall fall to the ground; all shall have its fulfillment in due time.[99]

Adam Clarke: Holiness Preacher

Throughout his preaching career, Dr. Adam Clarke was known to be a holiness preacher. From the beginning to the end, sanctification through the Spirit was Clarke's view and he preached it faithfully for fifty years. Although Adam Clarke is known to have preached thousands of sermons, he chose to write out very few of them. It was only towards the end of his life, and 'with great diffidence', that he published (in three volumes, 1828 to 1830) a collection of sixty-four sermons (under the general title 'Discourses on Various Subjects'). Out of the sixty-four, twenty were on the theme of holiness. He loved preaching and he was in his element when in the pulpit. Regarding the twenty, Adam was certain that when Christ came into the soul, he began to sanctify and to cleanse the soul from all defilement. Christ came in and the believer's heart was purified from all its sin. These twenty sermons will be the theme of this chapter.

The first of these twenty (Sermon VI of the series) is based on Philippians 1:9-11 and is headed, 'Experimental Religion and its Fruits'. Clarke reminds us that if we are in the right spiritual state, we can look to the same unchanging God through the Spirit, who is the same yesterday, today and for ever. We may claim the promises on this sure foundation and we will receive that engrafted word which is able to make us wise unto salvation.

> It is not enough that they are *saved from sin*, but they must be *filled with righteousness*…. He first casts out sin; this he can do in a moment…. but the filling of righteousness is a progressive work….; In a moment he may be emptied of sin, and…. a seed of righteousness be deposited…. Being emptied of all sin is a small matter, when compared with being filled with God….. It is the Spirit of Jesus Christ that witnesses with ours, that we are the children of God. It is his blood that cleanseth us from all unrighteousness. And it is by his dwelling in our hearts…. that we are rooted and grounded in love, and are filled with all the fullness of God…. We are accepted through him, because purchased by him; and finally glorified together with him…. Turn from every sin, give up every

---

[99]   Clarke, *Commentary*, Revelation 22:17-19.

idol, cut off every right hand, pluck out every right eye…. Thy day is far spent, the night is at hand…. and here thou hast no abiding city. A month, a week, a day, an hour, yea, even a moment, may send thee into eternity…. Remember then that nothing but the blood of Jesus can cleanse thee from all unrighteousness. Lay hold, therefore, on the hope that is set before thee, re-echo the apostle's prayer, and apply it to thyself. The gate may appear straight, but strive, and thou shalt pass through!…. Amen and Amen. [100]

Preaching on Ephesians 3:14-21 (Sermon XIII, 'The Family of God, and its Privileges', Adam Clarke postulates on the prayer for the church at Ephesus. His prayer is the most grand and sublime in the oracles of God. The prayer itself is the immediate inspiration from heaven and its incomparable language is the divine Spirit of that eternal measure through which he provided salvation for a lost world.

…he is led to view him in his unlimited power that he may appear to be justified in the extensive petitions he has made. Who can overthrow the power of sin but God? Who can pardon its guilt but God? Who can clean the human heart from all unrighteousness but God? Who can raise a body that is dead because of sin from death and corruption but God? Who can endue it with immortality, unite it to its proper spirit, but God? And who can bring both to his own everlasting glory, there to dwell eternally, but God?…. The song of praise to God through Christ, begun on earth and protracted through all the generations of men, till the end of time, shall be continued in heaven…. where, being like him, they shall see him as he is…. in which state, eras, limits and periods are absorbed in one eternal duration. [101]

Dr. Clarke on Matthew 22:35-40 (Sermon XXIII, 'Love to God and Man, the Fulfilling of the Law and the Prophets') starts with the love we owe to God and man. We are assured by our Lord himself that the whole of religion is comprised in this, loving God and our neighbour. It has nothing earthly, nothing animal or fleshly in it. It is a pure flame that has come from God, changing and refining our nature and returning all its ardour back to itself.

---

[100] Adam Clarke, *Discourses on Various Subjects relative to the Being and Attributes of God; and His Works , in Creation, Providence, and Grace* (4 vols., reprinted with General Preface by James Everett; London: T. Tegg & Son, 1836), Vol. 1, p.135 and pp.139-140; hereafter cited as 'Clarke, *Discourses*'.
[101] Clarke, *Discourses*, Vol. 1, p.297 and p.306.

He lives under the influences of the life-giving Spirit and increases daily in love both to God and man. The life of the wicked may be justly termed an ever-living death; but the life of the righteous is an ever-living life. He lives in death itself! Death is his; it is the gate of eternal life to his deathless spirit. He shall never die; and he lives where there is there is no death; he lives through eternity.... Behold, therefore, what manner of love the Father hath bestowed on us, that we should be called the sons of God! Father of mercies! God of light, power and love! illuminate, quicken and invigorate the minds of thy people; let them see the glorious hope of their calling.... And does he not know.... Then he must be this moment willing to cleanse us if he expects a loving obedience from us, which he knows is impossible till he has sprinkled clean water upon us, and made us clean? "The Spirit and the bride say, Come! and let him that is athirst come; and whosoever will, let him come, and take the water of life freely!"[102]

In Sermon 28 ('The Glory of the Latter Days'), Dr. Clarke preaches on Joel 2:28, 'I will pour out my spirit upon all flesh,' and states that every true Christian is hoping for better days. He hopes for better times in reference to a more extensive dissemination of the words of truth over the earth and a larger effusion of the Divine Spirit to make the enlargement of truth effectual to the salvation of men. In religious matters these hopes are expectations, and are founded upon the promises of God, reported by the holy writers, and to the glory of the Church made up of all its people from around the world.

Now the glory of the latter days is evidently the revelation of Christ, and the universal pouring out of his Spirit; for as he, by the grace of God, tasted death for every man (Heb. 2: 9); and his grace, which brings salvation to all men, hath appeared.... The Holy Spirit was "to convince the world of sin, righteousness and judgment".... Nor are we in any times to expect a greater or more efficacious Saviour than Jesus Christ; nor a more powerful and energetic Agent, than the Holy Ghost, the Spirit of judgment, and the Spirit of burning.... These are the times in which Christ offers to dwell in the hearts of all true believers by faith, that they may be rooted and grounded in love, and prove with all saints what is the length, and breadth, and depth, and height, and know the love of God that passeth knowledge, and be filled with all the fullness of God!.... Can our hearts be more than filled? Can our souls be filled with

---

[102] Clarke, *Discourses,* Vol. 2, pp.177-179.

more than all the fullness of God?.... Reader, lay these things to heart; now arise, and shake thyself from the dust..... Be not slothful to go and enter to possess the land. Awake, awake; put on thy strength, O Zion; put on thy beautiful garments, O Jerusalem, the Holy City....[103]

Dealing with 2 Peter 1:3, 4 (in Sermon XXX, 'The Corruption that in the World through Lust'), Dr. Clarke wrote of the moral state of society at the time to which Peter referred. The inscription appears to have special reference to those who were driven, through persecution, to seek refuge in those foreign lands. Some of them were converted Jews, others converted Gentiles, all suffering for righteousness sake and seeing to these laws according to the directions of the Lord: 'When they persecute you in one city, flee unto another.' As to their internal state, we are told, 'Chosen of God, through the sanctification of the Spirit, obedient to the truth of the gospel':

> Let none of the corrupt, those who through lust are under the influence of the spirit of the world, expect to enter into the kingdom of God. No man's creed, however orthodox will save him.... No passport to heaven, but Christ in the heart, the hope of glory.... circumcision is nothing and uncircumcision is nothing, but a new creation – the faith which works by love, and purifieth the heart. We must have a divine nature to go to a divine place. We are called by his glory and virtue - by his glorious power in us.... He works virtue, holiness and purity in us by the energy of his Spirit; and calls us to a future state of blessedness, by glory and virtue as exciting agents.... See that thou bring forth the fruits of that faith and love which thou already hast; and in the spirit of loving obedience, according to thy present means of grace, expect that fullness of God which He has promised. Nothing can withstand the conquering blood of Jesus; nothing, the sovereign energy of His almighty Spirit.[104]

Time and again Dr. Clarke turned to the fundamentals of the faith and wrote down what he considered to be the all-important question arising from 'Salvation by Faith', the title of his Sermon XXXIV, dealing with Acts 16:30 and the question: 'What must I do to be saved?' In this Sermon, Clarke has searched the Scriptures, and prayed for the succours of the Spirit of wisdom to spread it abroad to thousands of people. To spread the gospel through the world, God had

---

[103] Clarke, *Discourses*, Vol. 2, pp.320-322.
[104] Clarke, *Discourses*, Vol. 2, p.383 and p.385.

delivered the word to his people: 'Go ye into all the world and preach the gospel to every creature.'[105] The danger which faces any man or woman, is that of dying in a state of sin, and falling under the wrath of God. The cause of this danger is having sinned against God, and the jailer, in Acts 16, felt that Paul was telling him to escape and seek the Lord. Dr. Clarke preaches on this important text and he saves his fire until the end.

> This pardon and reconciliation, this holiness and purity, and this eternal glory, come all in consequence of the incarnation, passion, death, resurrection, ascension and mediation of Christ; and this complete restoration to the image and likeness of God is the utmost salvation the soul of man can possess.... no scheme of salvation ever invented by man can procure or produce these blessings;.... [and] we may confidently assert that "there is no name under heaven given among men whereby we must be saved...." (Acts 4: 12).... [and] .... he who receives salvation by faith receives, at the same time, power from God to live in obedience to every moral precept.... They are born of God, and his seed remaineth in them, and they cannot sin because they are born of God.... they have their fruit unto holiness, and the end is everlasting life.... Thus the grand original law is once more written on their hearts by the finger of God; and they are restored both to the favour and the image of their Maker. They love him with all their powers, and they serve him with all their strength.... They are saved from their sins, are made partakers of the divine nature, escape the pollutions that are in the world; and, being guided by his counsel, they are at last saved received up his glory.[106]

In Sermon XXXVIII (in his series of sixty-four *Discourses*), Dr. Clarke preached from Colossians 1:27, 28, and gives it the title 'Apostolic Preaching'. In the Shetlands Islands he saw much of the Lord's power, and he preached this sermon at Lerwick on June 18, 1826, and dedicated it 'To The Inhabitants Of The Zetlands Isles, And Particularly To The Members Of The Methodist's Societies In Those Islands, This Discourse Is Respectfully Inscribed By Their Firm And Affectionate Friend, Adam Clarke'. The sacred writers often sum up all their doctrines in a single verse and this the apostle does in verse twenty-seven. 'Christ in you, the hope of glory'.

---

[105] Mark 16:15.
[106] Clarke, *Discourses*, Vol. 3, pp.164-166.

In short, he proclaimed him [Christ] as Prophet, Priest and King; and as a complete Saviour from all the power of all sin; from all the guilt of sin; and from all the in-being and defilement of all sin.... Many talk much.... of what Christ has done FOR US: but how little is spoken of what he is to do IN US. He was incarnated, suffered, died, and rose again from the dead; ascended to heaven and there appears in the presence of God for us.... These were all saving, atoning and mediating acts for us; that he might reconcile us to God; that he might blot out our sins; that he might purge our consciences from dead works.... wash the polluted heart, destroy every foul and abominable desire.... fill the soul with his light, power and life, and, in a word, destroy the works of the devil.[107]

In this same sermon, Dr. Clarke expounds these verses and in reference to this, he has been given this gospel to preach, the glad tidings of salvation – that Christ came to restore men and women to the divine image and likeness, and this he does by destroying the power, pardoning the guilt and purifying from the defilement of sin.

Sin must have no triumph; and the Redeemer of mankind must have his glory. But if man be not perfectly saved from all sin, sin does triumph, and Satan exult, because they have done a mischief that Christ either cannot or will not remove.... When Christ casts out the strong-armed man, he takes away that armour in which he trusted, he spoils his goods: he cleanses and enters into the house, so that the heart becomes the habitation of God through the Spirit.... He was incarnated, suffered, died, and rose again from the dead that he might make an atonement for the world, and save his people from their sins.... We never properly know his worth, nor feel our obligation to him, till we feel that he has blotted out our sin, and healed the infected streams of our fallen nature.[108]

There have been angels who kept not their first estate; and we all know to our cost that he who was the head and fountain of the whole human race; who was made in the image and likeness of God, sinned against God and fell into that state. Faith must be kept in lively exercise, working by love; and that love is only safe when found exerting its energies in the path of obedience:

---

[107] Clarke, *Discourses*, Vol. 3, pp.266- 267.
[108] Clarke, *Discourses*, Vol. 3, p.277 and pp.286-287.

The truth is, no doctrine of God stands upon the knowledge, experience, faithfulness, or unfaithfulness of man; it stands on the veracity of God who gave it. If there were not a man to be found who was justified freely through the redemption that is by Jesus; yet the doctrine of justification by faith is true, for it is a doctrine that stands on the truth of God. And suppose not one could be found in all the churches of Christ whose heart was purified from all unrighteousness; and who loved God and man with all his regenerated powers; yet the doctrine of Christian perfection would still be true; for Christ was manifested that he might destroy the work of the devil; and his blood cleanseth from all unrighteousness.... I conclude…. that as Christ among and in the people, the hope of glory, was the sum and substance of the apostle's preaching; so, their redemption from ALL sin, its power, guilt, and contamination, even in this life, was the grand, the only end at which he aimed in all his ministry; and that to labour to present every man perfect in Christ Jesus, is at once, the duty and glory of every Christian preacher.[109]

Coming to Sermon XLII, 'True Happiness, and the Way to Attain it', we find Dr. Clarke writing this sermon on November 16, 1830. He takes Psalm 40:16-17, and concentrates on verse 17; 'Make no tarrying, O my God.' His great business is now to hold fast what he has received and to put all the energies into watching in the work of faith, the patience of hope and the labour of love. He may grow in grace as the soul grows in capacity and he perseveres because he is faithful. He is a branch of the true vine. Every believer should assume the motto, Believe, Love, Obey. Nothing can separate him from the love of God in Christ: neither death, nor life, nor angels, nor principalities, nor powers, nor things present, nor things to come, nor height, nor depth, nor any other creature. The glory of the Lord is risen upon him; let him stand fast in the liberty wherewith Christ has made him free. As Dr. Clarke puts it:

….the persons in the text who are filled with the fullness of God, are called to magnify the Lord, in showing particularly that the "blood of Christ cleanseth from all unrighteousness," - that Jesus saveth to the uttermost, - that he will save believers from all sin in this life.... He has all power in the heavens and the earth. He came into the world to save men and women from their sins.... and stamping the whole with the true, holy, and righteous image of the invisible God.... Both his justice and

---

[109] Clarke, *Discourses*, Vol. 3, pp.292-293.

mercy are magnified, in the proclamation, that Jesus Christ died for all men;…. that the ransom price is paid down for every human soul; and that all may be saved…. Hallelujah! Save now, O Lord, we beseech thee! O Lord, send now prosperity![110]

Out of the sixty-four sermons in Dr. Adam Clarke's *Discourses*, one quarter is devoted to what the risen Lord does in the soul of a believer. We have noted that about three quarters of these sermons deal with the place where Christ dwells in the human heart and displays his glory. The last two sermons were delivered in the months that followed, and the last one was preached about a month before Dr. Clarke died. This sermon (LXIII, 'God's Love in Jesus Christ, Considered in its Objects, its Freeness, and Saving Results'), was preached before the Anniversary meeting of the Wesleyan Missionary Society in Great Queen Street, London, April 27, 1832, and was based upon the words of 1 John 3:1, 2. These words from 1 John, chapter 3, are all about that love which requires our attention, our almost fixed attention, that God will open our hearts that we may understand the Scriptures and see the power and influence of his Holy Spirit. There was a time when God considered the priority of making man - and he was made holy, pure, in union with his Maker. He knew no sin, no evil passion, there was no erring judgment, all was right, all was just and true and holy. Dr. Clarke finds his subject – the great love and redemption that is in Christ Jesus:

> ….he has done this in order that you might become his sons, the children of the Almighty, be readmitted into the family of heaven…. and that, though you have fallen, deeply fallen…. you might yet become glorious in holiness, capable not only of knowing him, but of dwelling *in* him and *with* him to all eternity…. Oh, blessed plan! Oh, wondrous - Oh, astonishing plan!…. was it a small thing that he, in whom dwelt all the fullness of the Godhead bodily, should be manifested in the flesh,…. should assume the likeness of man, and humble himself, and become obedient unto death, even the death of the cross? Oh, greatest of all miracles! that Christ should die at all…. this most holy Jesus, this God manifest in the flesh, died to take away our sins.[111]

---

[110] Clarke, *Discourses*, Vol. 3, pp.439- 440.
[111] Clarke, *Discourses*, Vol. 4, pp.380-381.

As Dr. Clarke pondered these things, he was thinking of these mysteries and marvelled that all those that heard him were younger than he was:

> My brothers and sisters, believe an old man, who has studied this matter longer, perhaps, than any or most of you have lived. Believe him, after having tried by every rule of reason of which he is a master, he is obliged to come to this - that there can be no genuine happiness on this side of heaven…. unless God has a testimony to give to the conscience of man, that he, in mercy, has been brought into God's wondrous love…. and is united to the family of heaven….. This is what the apostle insists upon – "Beloved, now," says he, "are we the sons of God." We are called to this state of salvation – we have found the pearl of great price…. This is what I wish you not to rest without. Do not face death without it. Do not! It is an awful thing to appear before the living God, if you have not the testimony in your souls that you are born of him…. It is very likely that this old man may not plead with you again. He would have no objection to live until God's appearance on the earth, and till the archangel trumpet sounded, to promote the glory of God as his greatest delight, and to bring souls to love that God that loves him, and to love that Jesus who died for him…. He will delight in the widow that brings her mite, and in the rich man who brings his store, into the treasury of the Lord, to assist his cause and extend it in the world.[112]

We have come at last to Sermon LXIV, the sixty-fourth and final message of Adam Clarke's *Discourses*. It was preached, just a month before he died, at Stanhope Street Chapel, Wesley Place, Liverpool, on the morning of August 5, 1832. Dr. Clarke had preached thousands of sermons, but only sixty-four of these were published in this approved way. The sermon has the title 'The Doctrine of Repentance', and is based on Acts 3:19, 'Repent you, therefore, and be converted, that your sins may be blotted out.' Dr. Clarke stood there, an old man with grey hair, ready to preach a sermon that will last. This address will prove to be a lasting sermon for, he stated, 'It is impossible, in any nation of the world where the doctrine [of salvation from all sin] is preached, that the people can lose their religion; or that it ever can be said, that the revival of religion, once among the Methodists, has ceased so many year hence.'[113] While the Methodists continued with its doctrine,

---

[112] Clarke, *Discourses*, Vol. 4, p.385 and pp.391-392.
[113] Clarke, *Discourses*, Vol. 4, p.396.

Clarke maintained, the work of God will increase and with so many calls to repentance a revival of religion must continue:

> Let us give God an occasion this morning.... to send down times of refreshing upon this place, [and to] give him an opportunity of displaying his boundless mercy.... If any of you begin to think it is all over with you, - no, no: why, there is a Saviour before the throne: but the time may come when it will be all over with you – but it is not so yet. 'I saw,' said the apostle, 'a lamb, newly slain, before the throne.' What a wonderful thing was that! Even at this time Christ Jesus had been raised from the dead, after his sacrificial atonement, a hundred years, and yet the apostle saw him, just as if newly slain. This is the whole secret of a mediatorial kingdom, and of the.... intercession of Jesus Christ. We have only to look to Jesus, and we see the continual reason why God, through the lapse of time, should save souls, seeing that Christ appears before the throne, as a lamb newly slain, actually now representing his pouring out the sacrificial blood, as a satisfaction, atonement, and oblation sufficient for the sins of the whole world![114]

Dr. Clarke feels that his time may be over but he is unwilling to leave his people so early. In less than a month he will be dead and then the Methodists will have to talk about him as one who is gone. Dr. Clarke ponders and wonders and has memories about his preaching. There were larger crowds that attended such meetings as Dr. Clarke's, and he just cannot stop with them on the road to heaven.

> You see, my friends, I am unwilling to leave you – I am unwilling to give up till I feel in my own mind satisfied, that I have succeeded in persuading you to come to God through the Son of his love. Take this further consideration to encourage you – that we may get all the fullness of the gospel – those who have not yet the witness of the Spirit, but have repented, may get it this morning; and those who have got it through the redemption that is in Christ Jesus, but who mourn because there is anything in their hearts that is not according to the will of God, and want it taken away, may have their hearts cleansed by the inspiration of the Holy Spirit, that 'they may perfectly love and worthily magnify God's holy name.' Here, then, is a mighty work of God - his Spirit knocks at the door of your hearts - open and let him in, and he will abide with you for ever.... He will be with you even at the hour of death, and conduct your souls into his immediate presence, where there is fullness of glory and pleasure for evermore. Oh, then, open the door of faith, and

---

[114] Clarke, *Discourses*, Vol. 4, pp.409-410.

lay hold on the hope set before you in the gospel! May God give you and me a wise understanding in these things, for Christ's sake! Amen.[115]

There were in the Christian Church plenty of those Christians who maintained a view of Scripture that advocated a 'second blessing'; a blessing of the Spirit in the Christian life. They were headed by John Wesley, Charles Wesley, John Fletcher, and Adam Clarke, and by a host of others up to the present day. However, during the early 1960s, three books were published in America that questioned the position of Dr. Adam Clarke. The first (in 1962) was called, *Insights into Holiness*,[116] and it presented papers by fifteen scholars who outlined the position of purity in the light of God. That was followed (in 1963) by *Further Insights into Holiness*,[117] which was a further compilation of papers, this time by nineteen scholars who traced the doctrine of holiness through the centuries. The first book, on its title page, reckoned to have contributions from 'fifteen leading scholars of the Wesleyan persuasion.'[118] The compilation declared on its title page that readers would find within that 'Nineteen leading Wesleyan scholars present various phases of holiness thinking.'[119] The third compilation was entitled, *The Word and the Doctrine*,[120] and the title page maintained that it represented 'studies in contemporary Wesleyan-Arminian theology.' All three books made mention of Adam Clarke, but only two mention him by name.

George Failing from, *Insights Into Holiness*, in his article, 'Development in Holiness Theology After Wesley', writes about Clarke's definition of holiness:

---

[115] Clarke, *Discourses*, Vol. 4, pp.410-411.
[116] Kenneth Geiger, comp., *Insights into Holiness: Discussions of holiness by fifteen leading scholars of the Wesleyan persuasion*, Kansas City, Missouri: Beacon Hill Press, 1962; hereafter cited as 'Geiger, ed., 1962'.
[117] Kenneth Geiger, comp., *Further Insights into Holiness: Nineteen leading Wesleyan scholars present various phases of holiness thinking*, Kansas City, Missouri: Beacon Hill Press, 1963; hereafter cited as 'Geiger, ed., 1963'.
[118] Geiger, ed., 1962.
[119] Geiger, ed., 1963.
[120] Kenneth E. Geiger, comp., *The Word and the Doctrine: Studies in contemporary Wesleyan-Arminian theology*, Kansas City, Missouri: Beacon Hill Press, 1965; hereafter cited as 'Geiger, ed., 1965'.

70

It may be surprising that this theological balance was early threatened – we might say, was early thrown off centre – and that by Methodism's first theologian, Adam Clarke.... Mr. Clarke, though a scholar in languages, was essentially an evangelist in doctrines. His book, *Christian Theology,* neatly packages and labels the various doctrines.... Clarke emphasized almost exclusively the instantaneous phase of sanctification and quite neglected the growth phase, writing: 'In no part of the Scriptures are we directed to seek holiness *gradatim* (gradually, step by step). We are to come to God as well for an instantaneous and complete purification from all sin, as for an instantaneous pardon. Neither the *gradatim* pardon or the *seriatim* purification exists in the Bible.'.... 'This perfection is the restoration of man to the state of holiness from which he fell, by creating him anew in Jesus Christ, and restoring to him that image and likeness of God which he has lost.... Turn from every sin, give up every idol, cut off every right hand, pluck out every right eye.... Thy day is far spent, the night is at hand.... A month, a week, a day, an hour, yea, even a moment may send thee into eternity. And if thou die in thy sins, where God is thou shalt never come. Do not expect redemption in death.... The gate may appear strait; but strive and thou shalt pass through.... Hear his voice, believe at all risks, and struggle into God.'[121]

This is a serious argument against Adam Clarke – if it can be proved. Dr. Clarke did not write a systematic theology, but his writings on all the major Christian doctrines were collected from his various writings and published two years after his death. It will be seen at once that Dr. Clarke is arguing concerning the *initial* cleansing, not the subsequent development, but apart from that, the paragraph must be taken with the whole essay. Clarke was replying to those who believed only in a gradual work and denied the instantaneous; he was also replying to those who believed, but were careless in their efforts to obtain this blessing. All through the essay there is a great insistence on putting aside every excuse and hindrance. Clarke's whole approach is the most passionate plea on this issue that one has read. He certainly insisted on the instantaneous aspect but Clarke did not deny the gradual work in the soul, as can be seen in his words:

---

[121] George Failing, 'Developments in Holiness Theology After Wesley', in Geiger, ed., 1962, pp.14-16.

Increase in the image and favour of God. Every grace and divine influence which ye have received is a seed, a heavenly seed, which, if it be watered with the dew from heaven above, will endlessly increase and multiply itself. He who continues to believe, love and obey, will grow in grace and continually increase in knowledge of Jesus Christ, as his Sacrifice, Sanctifier, Counsellor, Preserver and final Saviour. The life of a Christian is a growth: he is at the first born of God, and is a little child: becomes a young man and a father in Christ.... In order to get a clean heart, a man must know and feel its depravity, acknowledge and deplore it before God....[122]

Does that sound like someone who, according to Failing, 'quite neglected the growth phase'? It is significant that in Failing's criticism only part of Clarke's paragraph is quoted. Two paragraphs further on Clarke adumbrates on the passion of our Lord:

As the blood of Jesus Christ, the merit of his passion and death, applied by faith, purges the conscience from all dead works, so the same cleanses the heart from all unrighteousness. As all unrighteousness is sin, so he that is cleansed from all unrighteousness is cleansed from all sin. To attempt to evade this, and plead for the continuance of sin in the heart through life, is ungrateful, wicked, and blasphemous.... Reader, it is the birthright of every child of God to be cleansed from all sin, to keep himself unspotted from the world, and so to live as never more to offend his Maker.[123]

This is hardly an 'outright repudiation of the gradual.' Dr. Failing further asserts that Clarke 'included a bit too much in his claim for perfection.' Failing cites Clarke as writing: 'This perfection is the restoration of man to the state of holiness from which he fell.... by restoring to him that image and likeness of God which he had lost.' Failing then asks: 'Is indeed that total image recovered now? Adam Clarke does not sufficiently explain this.'[124] Again Clarke has been quoted without respect to his whole essay. Because Clarke claimed for

---

[122] [Adam Clarke], *Christian Theology: by Adam Clarke, LL.D., F.A.S. selected from his published and unpublished writings, and systematically arranged: with a life of the author.* ed. Samuel Dunn, Second Edition [May 1835]. London: Thomas Tegg & Son, 1835, p.230; hereafter cited as 'Clarke, ed. Dunn, 1835'.

[123] Clarke, ed. Dunn, 1835, p.231. (Also in Clarke, ed. Dunn, repr., 1967, 204.)

[124] George Failing, 'Developments in Holiness Theology After Wesley', in Geiger, ed., 1962, pp.15-16.

perfection no more than John Wesley, whose favourite description was, 'The image of God stamped upon the heart.'[125] Clarke never used the word 'total image' but he did write:

> The whole design of God was to restore man to his image, and raise him from the ruins of his fall; in a word, to make him perfect; to blot out all his sins, purify his soul, and fill him with holiness.... The truth is, no doctrine of God stands upon the knowledge, experience, faithfulness, or unfaithfulness of man; it stands on the veracity of God who gave it.... And suppose not one could be found in all the churches of Christ whose heart God was purified from all unrighteousness, and who loved God and man with all his regenerated powers; yet the doctrine of Christian perfection would still be true; for Christ was manifested that He might destroy the work of the devil....[126]

There is much more on this theme in the essay. Surely Clarke does 'sufficiently explain' what he meant by Christian perfection, and if he be charged with including 'a bit too much' then the same charge must equally be levelled at Wesley and Fletcher. Adam Clarke was far too careful a scholar and exegetic to ever write of a restoration of the 'total image' of God in this life while the understanding is ignorant of a thousand things and the body, even for the most saintly believer, is dead because of sin. In this present defence of Clarke, quotations have been restricted to his essay, 'Entire Sanctification' (in his *Christian Theology*), but the criticism made against him by Failing could easily be answered further from Clarke's *Commentary* and his sermons.

Hollis Abbott writes of the 'tremendous influence in holiness circles of Adam Clarke, who recognized only the instantaneous aspect of Christian perfection and ruled out the gradual and the effect he had on the people who followed.'[127] However, it is difficult to tell whether Abbott has spent time with Clarke, because to back what he says, instead of citing Clarke directly, Abbott merely quotes from John L. Peters who appears to believe that Clarke, 'In his treatment of perfection the almost exclusive emphasis upon it [*sic*] instantaneous phase and his outright repudiation of the gradual pointed the way for

---

[125] For example see Sermon 45, 'The New Birth', in: Wesley, *Works* [BE], Vol. 2, p.195.
[126] Clarke, ed. Dunn, 1835, p.207 and p.216.
[127] Hollis F. Abbott, 'Christian Maturity', in Geiger, ed., 1965, p.302.

the more extreme wings of Wesleyan perfectionism which were to follow.'[128]   In all these three writers (Failing, Abbott, and Peters) sufficient warrant has now been given to show that, if Adam Clarke's own wider writings are carefully read, he will be found to be exonerated from the charge made against him regarding his understanding of Christian perfection.

Adam Clarke and his Letters

Adam Clarke loved letter writing and all his years were filled with writing and remembering. As Adam grew older, his faith in people deepened and he often goes back in memory to catch people and places. In all his ministry he noted persons and places of worship, and he revelled in writing about them. Until his death he went round his circuits, and he loves telling people of his first visit to them. The number of his letters must be in the thousands, and all we can do now is to remember where and how he knew people over a long time.

One long letter stands out. It is when Adam Clarke wrote to John Wesley giving an account of what was happening in the Isle of Alderney. It is one preacher and minister pastor writing to another, and Adam thought the world of John Wesley and how he had devoted his long life to preaching, teaching and travelling.

> Guernsey, March 16, 1787.
> Rev. and very dear Sir,
> As in my last I intimated my intention to visit the Isle of Alderney; I think it my duty to give you some particulars relative to the success of that voyage.... I found [in a poor cottage] an old man and woman, who, having understood my business, bade me 'welcome to the best food they had,…. [and] to their house to preach in.' On hearing this, I saw plainly that the hand of the Lord was upon me for good, and I thanked them and took courage.... I told them I would preach that evening…. and long before the appointed hour…. I spoke of the kingdom of God, nearly as long as the little strength held out.... I then retired to my little apartment…. when the good woman…. came and entreated me to *come down and preach again*.... Deep attention sat on every face, while I shewed the great need…. of a Saviour, and exhorted them to turn

---

[128] Slightly misquoted by Abbott from: John Leland Peters, *Christian Perfection and American Methodism*, Nashville: Abingdon Press, 1956, p.107.

immediately from all their iniquities to the living God.... The next Sabbath morning, being invited to preach in the English church, I gladly accepted it, and in the evening I preached in the large warehouse at the Bray.... Many came together in the evening, to whom I again preached with uncommon liberty.... This, with several other observable circumstances, induced me to believe that my detention was of the Lord, and that I had not before fully delivered His counsel.... I recommended them to God, promised them a preacher shortly, and setting sail, I arrived in Guernsey.... Glory be to God for ever!.... an effectual door is opened in that Island for the reception of the everlasting Gospel, and am convinced I did not mistake the call of the Lord. One thing I believe greatly contributed to the good that may have been done: *viz.* a day of fasting and prayer, which I got our Societies both in town and country to observe. Were this method more frequently adopted we should not attempt the introduction of the Gospel so much in vain. There is not the smallest opposition nor even the appearance of any....

I am, Rev. and Dear Sir,

Your Affectionate and Obedient Son in the Gospel,

Adam Clarke. [129]

When Adam Clarke was in London, he acquired lots of books, and he was always on the look-out for important sales. While he was there, an important catalogue with books belonging to the Rev. Mr. Fell, Principal of the Dissenting College at Hackney, came to him and he noticed a black-letter Bible. The sale was on the day for a Quarterly-meeting for Methodists, so Adam found a buyer who was willing to bid for him. When the meeting ended, Clarke went to Paternoster Row and found the book was waiting for him. It was a rare 14th century manuscript 'black-letter' Wycliffe translation Bible, and Adam wrote the following in the fly-leaf:

This *Bible*, the first translation into the English language, and evidently, from the orthography and diction, the oldest copy of that translation, was once the property of *Thomas a' Woodstock*, youngest son of Edward III, King of England, and brother to *Edward* the *Black Prince*, and *John of Gaunt....* In many respects the language of this MS. is older than that found in most of those copies which go under the name of *John Wiclif.* This MS. was once in the possession of the celebrated Dr. *John Hunter.* It was found in a most shattered condition, and from the hay and bits of mortar that were in it...., hid, probably during the *Maryan Persecution*,

---

[129] *Account*, Vol. 1, p.272ff.

in stacks of hay, and at other times built up in walls, and not unfrequently, it would appear, that it had been secreted under ground, as was evidenced from the decayed state of many of its pages, especially the early ones.[130]

Following his time in the Channel Islands, two letters from Adam Clarke (to Robert Carr Brackenbury, dated January 3 and June 15, 1790) give details of his new exhausting ministerial activities now in Bristol.

For about a month [around December 1789] I have been employed in visiting the classes: this close work has proved more than I could well sustain: I need not say that preaching three or four times a-day, and giving out tickets to two hundred or three hundred people, regulating the spiritual concerns of the visitation of the society, &c., is more than any common strength is able to perform: from what I now feel, and the increase of the work, I have every reason to believe that I shall be either in eternity before Conference, or be fully invalided.... I see such fruit of my labour as causes me almost to rejoice in the martyred body which the most merciful God has, in his condescension, made an honoured instrument in helping forward so good a work. [On June 15, 1790, Clarke writes].... To reduce preaching into the rules of science, and to learn the art of it, is something of which my soul cannot form too horrid an idea. I bless Jesus Christ I have never learned to preach, but, through his eternal mercy, I am taught from time to time by him as I need instruction.... I read a good deal, write very little, but strive to study.[131]

In a letter to Mr. Alexander Mather, dated Manchester, December 23, 1791, Adam Clarke mentions some recurring health issues:

....I feel it a duty I owe to gratitude, to God, to inform you of it, and to make you a partaker of my consolations, as I have made you a sharer of my sorrows. Through the abundant kindness of God, my health seems better that it has been for some years.... [After preaching three times] The next day I was very bad; but in three or four days, through God's goodness I got well again.... There is a good work among the people. Many are stirred up to seek *purity of heart*; and two men, at our last public bands, gave a clear, rational account of a complete deliverance from all evil tempers and desires.... They have enjoyed this glorious liberty for about two months.... [and] it is a great encouragement for me

---

[130] *Account*, Vol. 2, pp.30-32.
[131] Hare, 1842, p.87.

to proceed in my work.... I look on this doctrine as the greatest honour of Methodism and the glory of Christ. God Almighty forbid that it should ever cease among us![132]

In Leeds, July 28, 1806, a reluctant Adam Clarke was named President of the Conference, and in a letter about a week later to his wife, he reports that Thomas Taylor and Joseph Bradford 'lifted me out of my seat' and placed him upon the table. In it he tells Mary Clarke about the experience and what had been happening at the Conference:

....I went to the chapel half an hour before the time, and finding it excessively filled, I immediately began. I first sang, than prayed, and afterwards called over the names of the seventeen young preachers to know if all were present.... I called upon each by his name to give an account of his conversion to God, and his call to the Christian ministry; and each did so with a precision and excellence, which did honour both to themselves and to us.

When this was ended, we sang *Praise God from whom all blessings flow, &c.* Mr. Thomas Taylor then gave them a charge, which, for about eight minutes, he did with a great feeling and excellence. I then addressed them in a short speech, and pronounced the form of reception in the name of God, whose mercy and love they were to proclaim; - in that of Jesus Christ whose atonement they were to witness; - in that of the Holy Ghost, by whose influence they were.... to be instrumental in alarming, convincing, converting, and in holiness building up the souls of men: - also in the name of the Methodist Conference, by whose authority I acted; and in the name of the many thousands which constitute that Church connected with them; - I thus admitted them into Full Connexion and union with the whole body of itinerant preachers! Much solemnity rested on the whole assembly. Mr. Moore then prayed, and I pronounced the dismissal. Preachers and people seemed exceeding pleased.... I believe I have acquitted myself to the satisfaction of the brethren, and I feel that I have acted with entire uprightness towards my God.... You know, my dear Mary, that there never was any love lost between us. Yourself and the children are all I have on this side the God of heaven. I will see you as soon as I can.... to take you by the hand as my everlasting wife; so says,
Your Affectionate Husband,
Adam Clarke.[133]

---

[132] Hare, 1842, pp.104-5.
[133] *Account*, Vol. 2, pp.96-7.

As soon as the British and Foreign Bible Society was formed in London in 1804, Dr. Clarke was anxious to give it all the help he could. He published a New Testament in Greek, with the modern and the ancient Greek printed in parallel columns. Adam assisted Professor Lee in completing a Syriac New Testament, and for this work he was presented with a gift of £50. He returned it to them and thanked them in the following letter, written June 20, 1807:

> ....With great respect and gratitude I return the *Fifty Pounds* which have been kindly sent me by the Committee of the British and Foreign Bible Society. To no principle from whence my services proceeded, to no feeling of my heart can I reconcile the acceptance of the Society's bounty. What I have done was for the sake of God and his truth; and I feel myself greatly honoured in having a part in this blessed work, and only regret that I have but a short time to devote to so useful an employment.... Have the goodness to assure the Committee of my perfect readiness.... to promote, as far as my time and abilities will permit, the great objects of this most benevolent association, which like the apocalyptic angel, is flying through the midst of heaven, having the everlasting Gospel to preach to every nation, and kindred, and people, and tongue. With best respects to the Committee, I am, Gentlemen, Your very affectionate fellow-labourer in the British and Foreign Bible Society, Adam Clarke.[134]

When Adam Clarke's *Commentary* was published, there was quite a number who wrote encouragingly about the work but there were some who blamed Clarke for missing out the decrees to those 'elected' to be saved. On October 22, 1810, he wrote a letter to the Rev. J. H., explaining that a man may be firm in his own belief, and yet destitute of bitterness towards others who hold a different doctrine:

> Dear Sir,
> I now take up your Letter which.... I only received about half an hour ago. I can say, in the fear of God, that I studied in every part of the work in question, to avoid every expression which might give offence or pain to any man.... Either I have been misinformed, or I took it for granted, that all Calvinists in *England*, were against what we call, the *decree of unconditional reprobation*, and I really thought that I should displease no person by simply stating what I did, and I thought I had done in as mild and dispassionate a way as possible.... My dear Friend, permit me

---

[134] *Account*, Vol. 2, pp.115-6.

to say that, when the Calvinists in general, speak of the Methodists, they do it without ceremony; in many cases with cruelty, and, as I have myself witnessed, in absolute hostility to truth. Might not a Methodist, who is far from wishing to make any reprisals, say, without offence, that they hold certain doctrines, without stating that they are either false or unjust.... I never wrote a Controversial Tract in my life: I have seen with great grief the provokings of many.... But my love of peace, and detestation of religious disputes induced me to keep within my shell, and never to cross the waters of strife....

At present I am greatly worn down by severe affliction, both in my own person and in my family.... As to myself, I find I must withdraw from public life. I have been able to do but little, and that little I can do no longer.... Begging an interest in your prayers, which I assure you I shall highly prize, I am, with best respects to Mrs. H., my dear Friend,
Yours affectionately,
Adam Clarke.[135]

Dr. Clarke left Dublin on July 16, 1812, reaching London on July 25, finding his son Theodoret still unwell, but gradually returning to health. In his *Journal* he recorded what he had found at various places:

....My son being in part restored to health, and having been desired by His Majesty's Commissioners to proceed to *Oxford* for the purpose of collecting papers for the Foedera, I have reached.... [Oxford], and today (Aug. 5), waited upon the Rev. Mr. Gaisford, Regius Professor of Greek in Christ Church, and delivered to him the Speaker's letter. He received me very politely, and promised every assistance in examining the *Bodleian* library, of which he is *curator*.

Aug. 6. - I went to my examinations, and afterwards, by Mr. Gaisford's invitation, dined in Hall at Christ Church. After dinner, I spent two hours with him very agreeably in the common room. It was no small gratification to a Methodist preacher to dine, and to sit on the same seat, and eat at the same table, where Charles Wesley, student of this college, often sat and dined: and where that glorious work, by the instrumentality of which some millions of souls have been saved, had its commencement, in conjunction with Mr. John Wesley, of Lincoln College. Oh, what hath God wrought since the year 1737.[136]

---

[135] *Account,* Vol. 2, pp.227- 231.
[136] *Account,* Vol. 2, pp.297-8.

In 1816, Dr Clarke travelled to Ireland in order to preside at the Irish Methodist Conference. Following this, touring the north of Ireland with two friends, he reached the place where he had been brought up. No place on earth was like this for Adam Clarke where he spent his boyhood for it had 'everything to recommend it to his attention and heart.' In his Journal he wrote that it was:

> ....where I first felt conviction of sin, righteousness, and judgment; where I first saw or heard a Methodist; where I first tasted the pardoning love of God, after having passed through a great fight of affliction; where I joined the Methodist Society; where I first led a class; where I first began to preach redemption in Christ Jesus, and from which I was called to become an itinerant preacher. And these things took place in the parish.... which is on the edge of the sea, where there is the most beautiful shore in the world, extending above twenty miles.... the very place where I was once drowned, and perhaps *miraculously* restored to life.... Such a place, thus circumstanced, must afford a multitude of the most impressive reminiscences. No place on the face of the earth can have so many attractions for me.[137]

Not long after, and back in England, Dr. Adam Clarke heard how a relative by marriage, Mr. Hugh Stuart Boyd, wanted to object against Methodism popularizing the doctrine of Christ's eternal judgment with the Father. He and Mr. Boyd generally got on well with each other but when Mr. Boyd wanted to publish a tract against Methodism, Clarke replied in a letter to Boyd that Methodism feared no foe, adding:

> I am as much surprised as you, to find that any of our preachers 'should labour hard to dissuade you from publishing your pamphlet against Methodism;' for, although I have a very high respect for your learning and abilities, I am sure that *Methodism has nothing to fear from anything that you or any other person can write on the subject in question*. The most subtle casuists in the land have long done what they could; and Methodism continues now, as it was then, as inexpugnable as the pillars of the eternal hills.... It has most sovereignly confuted all the arguments and calumnies ever brought against it; and, if you can bring anything new, worthy consideration, it will in all probability confute that also. You should bring forward no argument that has been answered; because this would expose you to the censure of writing on a subject which you did not understand; for we do not understand a

---

[137] Hare, 1842, p.179.

subject, if we are ignorant of what has been said or written *pro* or *con*....
Have you counted the cost, and answered to your own satisfaction the
cui bono? But I must not proceed, lest you should think that I also was
joining in the strong persuasives.... to prevent you from publishing....
Your very good friend,
Adam Clarke.[138]

In 1819 Adam Clarke was in Cornwall and staying at the home of Mr.
Mabyn in Camelford and he writes to his wife about what he calls his
'Preaching Expeditions'. On October 11 he writes about his visit to the
southern tip of Cornwall:

> *Land's End.* I write this, my dear Mary, in a situation that would make
> your soul freeze with horror: it is on the last projecting point of rock of
> the *Land's End*, upwards of 200 feet perpendicular above the sea, which
> is raging and roaring most tremendously, threatening destruction to
> myself and the narrow point of rock on which I am now sitting. On my
> right hand is the *Bristol* Channel, and before me the vast *Atlantic* Ocean.
> There is not one inch of land from the place on which my feet rest, to
> the vast *American* Continent! This is the place, though probably not so
> far advanced on the tremendous cliff, where *Charles Wesley* composed
> those fine lines:
>
> > 'Lo, on a narrow neck of land,
> > 'Twixt two unbounded seas I stand,' &c.
>
> The point of rock itself is about three feet broad at its termination, and
> the fearless adventurer will here place his foot, in order to be able to say,
> that he has been on the uttermost inch of land in the British Empire
> westward; and on this spot the foot of your husband now rests, while he
> writes the following words in the same hymn:
>
> > 'Oh, God my inmost soul convert,
> > And deeply on my thoughtful heart
> > Eternal things impress:
> > Give me to feel their solemn weight,
> > And tremble on the brink of fate,
> > And wake to righteousness.'
>
> I shall reserve the rest of my paper to be filled up in less perilous
> circumstances; so when you get this letter, you will know that I am
> safe.[139]

---

[138] Hare, 1842, p.180.
[139] *Account*, Vol. 2, pp.366-7.

The following letter was written by Adam Clarke in response to a letter received from the Rev. Mr. Hornby, Rector of Winwick, concerning the 'Direct Witness of the Spirit'. Dr. Clarke replied, saying he could find the witness in the experience of all true believers:

Millbrook, March 19, 1821.

....I should never had looked for the 'Witness of the Spirit,' had I not found numerous Scriptures which most positively asserted it, or held it out by necessary induction; and had not I found, that all the truly godly of every sect and party, possessed the blessing, - a blessing which is the common birth-right of all the sons and daughters of God. Wherever I went among deeply religious people, I found this blessing. All who had turned from unrighteousness to the living God, and sought redemption by faith in the blood of the cross, exulted in this grace. It was never looked on by them as a privilege which some peculiarly favoured souls were blessed with; it was known from Scripture and experience to be the common lot of the people of God.... Perhaps I might with the strictest truth say that, during the forty years I have been in the ministry, I have met with at least forty thousand, who have had a clear and full evidence, that 'God, for Christ's sake, had forgiven them their sins,' 'the Spirit himself bearing witness with their spirits, that they were sons and daughters of God.' The number need not surprise you when you learn that, every Methodist preacher converses closely, and examines thoroughly, every member of his societies, concerning the work of God upon their souls, once every three months. This single point of their spiritual economy, gives them advantages to know and discern the operations of the Divine Spirit in the enlightening, convincing, converting, justifying, sanctifying, and building up of the souls of men, which no other system affords, and no other ministries in the same degree possess.... Man is a fallen spirit; his inward parts are very wickedness; in his fall, he has lost the image of God. Let God shine into such a heart: let him visit every chamber in this house of imagery.... and, put the case that there had not been one act of transgression; what must be his feelings who thus saw, in the only light that could make it manifest, the deep depravity of his heart! ....This was my case. I saw myself in the sight of God a fallen spirit, lying in the wicked one, totally ruined by the fall, needing all the salvation which God, manifested in the flesh, purchased by His agony and bloody sweat, His vicarious and all-atoning passion and death.... Oh, may God save me from ever more falling under the power of this death!

I am, with much respect,
Your affectionate humble Servant,
Adam Clarke.[140]

Towards the close of the year 1821, Dr. and Mrs. Clarke went to Epworth and Dr. Clarke would preach to them on Sunday. It was a special day for the birthplace of John Wesley had a great attraction for the Clarkes, and this letter to his youngest daughter, written on September 18, is an account of their visit:

My dear Mary Ann,
Your mother and I, continuing our first intention of visiting Epworth.... we set off in a chaise from Rochdale.... We arrived at Epworth at one o'clock. It is a long, mean, straggling village, without symmetry or form, and in itself wholly uninteresting. We were kindly received at the house of Mrs. Wilkinson, where every attention was shewn us; and were soon informed that the Rev. Mr. Nelson, Rector of Wroote, and curate of Epworth, had been to inform young Mr. Wilkinson, that 'hearing Dr. Clarke was about to visit Epworth, he supposed that he would like to see the parsonage-house which had been built by old Mr. Samuel Wesley, and that he should have much pleasure in shewing it to him.'.... We proceeded to the parsonage. I trod the ground with reverence, and with strong feelings of religious gratification.... [They] led us into every room and apartment of the house up and down. I was greatly delighted. The house is a large plain mansion, built of brick.... It is a complete old-fashioned family house, and very well suited for nineteen children.... Having ended the examination.... we were shown into the parlour.... We then proceeded to the church: this revived my reverential feelings; it is simple, very plain and clean. I went to the Communion Table, which is the same as in Mr. Wesley's time; and I ascended the pulpit; and while kneeling on the base, pronounced to all that were below, these words, '*He that believeth in the Son of God, hath the witness in himself.*' Having looked a little about on all things, we went into the church-yard to see a Sycamore tree, which was been planted by the hand of old Samuel Wesley.... We marked also old Mr. Wesley's tombstone. With the whole of this visit, your mother and myself were highly pleased.... [Continuing the account in a letter written at Nottingham on September 21, 1821, Adam Clarke wrote] I preached at Epworth on the morning of the 19th for their chapel.... After the evening's Sermon, I administered the Sacrament to about 150 communicants. The people all appeared

---

[140] *Account*, Vol. 2, pp.381-385.

pleased and edified; a more genuine, simple-hearted, affectionate people, I have rarely seen; your mother was quite delighted with them….

With love from your mother,

I am, your affectionate father,

Adam Clarke.[141]

On March 29, 1823, Dr. Clarke wrote from Manchester to his friend the Rev. Thos. Smith, who had asked Clarke for his opinion of 'bodies of divinity', that is books tending to be based on intricate philosophical speculations rather than the original Scriptures:

My dear Brother Smith,

Your Letter deserved the earliest notice I could take of it, and of it I have never lost sight, but I am obliged to write much, read much, and think about many things which only concern me in my official capacity as President of our Conference; added to this I have to travel and labour from the main cause. On your main question, my opinion may be given in a few words: *Bodies of Divinity* I do most heartily dislike: they tend to supersede the Bible; and, independently of this, they are exceedingly dangerous.... The only preaching worth anything, in God's account, and which the fire will not burn up, is that which labours to convict and convince the sinner of his sin, to bring him into contrition for it, to convert him from it; to lead him to the blood of the covenant that his conscience may be purged from its guilt.... and then to build him up on this most holy faith by causing him to pray in the Holy Ghost, and keep himself in the love of God, looking for the mercy of our Lord Jesus Christ.... Labour to bring sinners to God; should you by it bring yourself to the grave.... I have often thought God designed you for an itinerant preacher, a current flame of fire. You can bear with me: though a Methodist, I love you full as well as any of your Calvinistic friends either can or do; and am ever,

Your affectionate Brother in Christ,

Adam Clarke.[142]

Dr. Adam Clarke never lost interest in his work for the Shetland Islands and from its inception to his final hours upon earth, he was always working for their good. In a letter to Mrs. William Williams, on June 27, 1824, for her considerate attention and active exertions for

---

[141] *Account*, Vol. 2, pp.402-406.

[142] *Account*, Vol. 3, pp.36-38.

those islands, he expresses the importance of the mission itself and for the labours and confidence he had in their missionaries.

I feel gratitude to God, Madam, in finding that He has disposed such as yourself to help me to bear a burden which, without such assistance, would be an overmatch for my strength. From the commencement of the Shetland mission, it has been placed by my brethren under my care, and its wants and trials come all before me, and indeed are laid upon me. I have been a missionary myself, and in various places have, for between forty and fifty years, seen the work of the Lord. But a more effectual opening among a numerous, very destitute, and interesting people, I have never witnessed. The labours through which the missionaries have gone, and are still going, are almost incredible; but God mightily sustains them, preserves their lives and health, and makes them more than a general blessing.

….There are four missionaries labouring there, of the same spirit; - Messrs. Dunn, Raby, Lewis, and Thompson. They are now building a chapel and preachers' house, at Lerwick, and I have gone a begging through all my friends to cover this expense; the latter will be a rendezvous for the missionaries when they return from time to time from visiting the different islands.... I thank you, Madam, in the name of God, and of this people, for what you have already done. You take such an interest in my poor Shetlanders, that I know not adequately how to express my thankfulness.... The Bibles and Testaments which you purpose sending for the people, will be most acceptable; but suffer me to say, the larger the print, the better, as there are many old people not well furnished with spectacles. I am always glad to see your letters, for they bring me good news of precious gifts, or liberal devices from you. May the Lord Jesus lay his healing hand upon you, and save you and yours with all the power of an endless life. Amen.

I am, my dear Madam,
Your much obliged humble servant,
Adam Clarke.[143]

The period for the holding of the Annual Wesleyan Conference was near at hand, and the Hinde Street Circuit, in which Dr. Clarke was stationed, wanted to retain his ministerial services for longer, and therefore put him down as a Supernumerary. As a result Dr. Clarke objected and 'felt his mind strong to labour' and he felt that the title of a Supernumerary should not apply to him. Nevertheless, on July 20,

---

[143] *Account*, Vol. 3, pp.78-80.

1831, he received the following letter from the Rev. George Marsden, of the Stationing Committee, telling him that he was appointed as Supernumerary to that Circuit:

> Bristol, July 20, 1831.
> Dear Brother,
> The Friends in the Hinde Street Circuit, have sent a strong request for you to be put down for their Circuit, stating that they have reason to believe that some arrangement may be made, that they may still be favoured with your valuable ministry. Not having any directions from you respecting your wishes, you are at present appointed as Supernumerary to that Circuit. Please to inform me if you wish it to be altered, or what are your particular wishes on the subject of your appointment.
> I am, dear Brother,
> Yours affectionately,
> G. Marsden.[144]

Dr. Clarke was devastated when he heard the news. It is to be regretted that the Wesleyan Conference did not consult with Dr. Clarke. It is clear that he had been wounded in the house of his friends. Dr. Clarke replied four days later.

> Baywater, near London, July 24, 1831.
> My dear brother Marsden,
> I do not find it easy to answer your Letter. All I ever said to my good friends at Hinde Street was this: - 'Were I to become Supernumerary this year, I would not prefer any circuit in London to that in which I am.' I am not clear that I should become a Supernumerary this year; but this I must leave with my brethren. I did not go out of my own accord, I dreaded the call, and I obeyed through much fear and trembling, not daring to refuse, because I felt the hand of God mighty upon me.... I had for some years thought of finishing where I began; though that circuit is now divided into four or six: or in that circuit where the word of the Lord came first to me; and where I found the salvation of God that bought me! In that circuit I have been endeavouring to raise up circuit schools; – not Mission schools, as has been reported by those who should have known better, but schools in places where *no kind of instruction* was afforded to the many hundreds of totally neglected wretched children, who with their parents were without the words of salvation.... Hitherto these *schools* and *local preachers* have not cost

---

Account, Vol. 3, p.338.

one farthing to any *fund* or *institution* among the Methodists; nor ever shall while I have anything to do with them. I hope, from the kindness, not of 'our friends,' but of *my friends*, to be able to put something in the hands of the Conference to help these Schools, when my voice can be heard no more on the mountains of Ireland; and when my plans are ripe, I shall get the Conference to appoint those for trustees in whom they have confidence, and who will be faithful in God's House. So much is my strength brought down by my three or four months' labour in Ireland, and also in different parts in *England*, besides *Cheshire*, *Lancashire*, and *Yorkshire*, that I do not think I could comfortably, or without farther injury to my health, bear the confinement of Conference this year.

I am, my dear brother M.,
Yours affectionately,
Adam Clarke.[145]

The letter which Dr. Clarke wrote afterwards to the Rev. John Lewis showed how he was wounded because of his friends.

Pinner, Middlesex, 1831.

My dear Brother Lewis,

I thank you for your Letter, and for the information it imparts: I feel that I have been ill-used in that work which God called me to, and which Mr. Wesley with his own hands confirmed me in, – by their setting me down for a Supernumerary against remonstrances made to the President himself, Mr. G. Marsden. When I found how it was, without opening the paper containing the usual annuity given to the Superannuated preachers, on their becoming such, I returned it immediately, and told Mr. Stanley not to enter my name on the next preachers' plan.... You see, therefore, that though I am hurt, I have not taken that offence which causes me to stumble. My time is nearly done. I have worked hard, borne many privations, and suffered much hardship, for more than half a century, and was still willing to work: and as I could still work with the same energy and effect, for God continued to own my word, it was not well to throw me thus far beyond the working pale! God is righteous, and my soul bows before Him!

Poor Shetland, I have worked hard for thee; many a quire, many a ream of paper have I written to describe thy wants, and to beg for supplies.... which by letter I had solicited for thee! It is now 'almost done, and almost over.' May God raise thee up another friend that will be, if

---

[145] *Account*, Vol. 3, pp.338-340.

possible, more earnest and faithful, and at the same time more successful! And now I must say, may the HOLY TRINITY be thy incessant friend, oh, my poor Shetland! Amen.... You have had sore affliction: though it be now past, yet my heart aches for you: well, your present station is a healthy one, and I hope God will give the spirit of health to you, Sister Lewis, and the little ones: give my love to them.
Ever your affectionate Brother,
Adam Clarke. [146]

Although Dr. Clarke was deeply offended at what the Conference had done to him, yet he attended his final Conference just before his death and he was asked to preach!

One letter arrived from America and it contained a message that he would love to have answered. It came from the Board of Managers of the Missionary Society of the Methodist Episcopal Church of New York and was dated December 23, 1831. Dr. Clarke responded to the letter, saying that he was extremely gratified by the letter and for the honour conferred upon him.

Feb. 6, 1832.
Gentlemen and Rev. Brethren,
Having been absent in the West of England for a considerable time, your letter did not reach my hand till some weeks after its arrival. Your kind invitation to visit the United States was gratifying to me, and had I been apprised of your intention a few months earlier, I should most certainly have endeavoured to have met your wishes, and by doing so, I have no doubt I should have been both gratified and profited. But the warning is too short, and I am engaged so far both to England and Ireland on behalf of our Missionary cause, that I cannot by any substitute redeem those pledges. I had proposed also to have visited the Zetland Isles if possible; but as I had not pledged myself to this voyage, I could have waived my purpose in favour of America, to visit which I have been long waiting for an opening of Providence; I might add, that I should have wished to have had the appointment of our Conference for the voyage.
Now, although I feel a measure of regret that I am disappointed in this wished-for visit to the American Continent; yet I am far from supposing

---

[146] *Account*, Vol. 3, pp.340-342.

that there may not be a providential interference in the way. I am, as no doubt you have already learnt, an *old man*, having gone beyond *three-score years and ten*, and consequently not able to perform the labour of youth. You would naturally expect me to preach much; and this I could not do. One sermon in the day generally exhausts me; and I have been obliged to give up all evening preaching, as I found the night air to be peculiarly injurious to my health. My help therefore must have been very limited, and in many cases this would have been very unsatisfactory to the good people of the *United States*.

I respect, I wish well to your State, and I love your Church.... I would say to all, keep your doctrines and your discipline, not only in your church books and in your society rules, but preach the former without refining upon them.... Truly, truly do I wish you good luck in the name of the Lord.... and hearty thanks to each of you individually for the handsome and honourable manner in which you have framed your invitation, I have the honour to be, Gentlemen, and Rev. Brethren,

Your obliged humble servant,
And most cordial well-wisher,
Adam Clarke.[147]

About seven weeks before he died, Dr. Clarke, in closing a short journal about what proved to be his last visit to Ireland, wrote:

This terminates a journey remarkable for affliction, disappointment, and suffering. I went over to Ireland to work; I could do nothing, being called to suffer. My soul, hast thou learned any good lesson? Yes. What is it? It is this: that I have now such evidences of old age as I never had before.... But during my late detention and sufferings, have I repined against God or His providence? - felt that my lot was hard, and that I was not permitted by Him to do that work which was for His glory? No: I was only disappointed; and I endured the mortification without a murmur. I was enabled to bow my neck to His yoke, or lie at His footstool. I felt that He was doing all things well, that I was safe if in His hands.... The cholera was before me, behind me, round about me; but I was preserved from all dread. I trusted in the sacrificial death of Jesus: no trust is higher; and none lower can answer the end. - I have redemption through His blood; and I am waiting for the fullness of the blessing of the Gospel of Jesus.

---

[147] *Account*, Vol. 3, pp.362-365.

I feel a simple heart: the prayers of my childhood are yet precious to me; and the simple hymns which I sang when a child, I sing now with unction and delight…. May I live to Thee, die in Thee, and be with Thee to all eternity. Amen. - Adam Clarke.[148]

When Dr. Adam Clarke got to Liverpool for the Methodist Conference in July, 1832, he did not think that this one would be his last. The cholera was raging but Dr. Clarke was too busy to mind these things. The date on the letter is July 22nd, 1832.

My dear Mrs. Tomkins,

I got to Liverpool last evening; obliged to travel all night and all yesterday. My friends were looking out for me. I have been to hear Mr. Entwisle in Brunswick chapel, on 'All the promises of God are yea and amen.' I am got here in the very jaws almost of the cholera. The man-servant of this family took it, and his wife took it also. They have escaped with the skin of their teeth. The mistress of our charity-school in this chapel, where we hold our Conference, was taken last Saturday, and died in a few hours. Her sister, who came to minister to her, returned to her own house, was seized on the road, and was dead before twelve o'clock.... I am waiting the Divine determination. We expect a crowd of preachers.... Liverpool is full of this ruinous disease. Now, my dear Mrs. Tomkins, I commend you and yours to God, and the word of His grace, which is able to build you up, and give you all an inheritance among the saints in light.[149]

---

[148] Etheridge, pp.438-9.
[149] Etheridge, pp.434-5.

Addendum

There have been biographies written on Dr. Adam Clarke - but only one has emerged from Ireland. It was *Adam Clarke: Saint and Scholar* (1963) by a native of Co. Tyrone, the Rev. Robert Henry Gallagher (1881-1965). Now, fifty-three years later, it is time for another one to be published, this one also by an Irishman! I began reading Dr. Adam Clarke fifty years ago and at last I'm producing a life of Adam. Adam Clarke has intrigued and fascinated me all these years and, apart from the fact that both of us have Irish parents, his faith and trust and amazing Bible scholarship have fired my imagination. The months spent in learning about him have been fascinating and all I've learned these past fifty years has been exciting. Dr. Adam Clarke has been one of the most outstanding preachers and scholars that have emerged in Methodism in Ireland, and my hope is that in reading this book you too will find him fascinating.

Appendix

This appendix contains images of a letter written by Dr Adam Clarke on January 2nd 1827. It came into the possession of the author when material was being collected in anticipation of his one day writing the present book; it is believed that this letter has not before been published or transcribed.

Adam Clarke's letter of January 2nd 1827, page one

or lie in their clothes among straw, &c. Of the arrival of those articles, I have not yet heard. I got them in Manchester & Stockport, & they were shipd from London for Leith & Lerwick. — I wish all the Preachers & their wives to be as comfortable as possible; & I am sure I have laboured incessantly, to afford them all the help in my power.

You delight me with the acc.t of your Schools—The Rrn. must divide largely with you, the Books which I have mentiond above. Lerwick is not the most necessitous place—Where the greatest want is, there let the greatest grace abound. I wish to know whether any of our good women have lost husbands, in the deaths, in the late Greenland fishery. If there be, let me know them, their necessity, & their children. The help that I got, & sent to the 5 widows & 22 children, I hope has been long since rec.d & applied. ——

The old woman left a noble Testimony—I will send this to the present month's mag. —

Watch my d.r Br.r while you have the light preach Jesus, & the blood of his cross. — the necessity of the broken & contrite heart—Salvation by faith—the witness of the Spirit, & redemption from all Sin. Tell the people that while evil tempers remain, they cannot be cleansed from all unrighteousness. Teach them to be

Adam Clarke's letter of January 2nd 1827, page two

93

diligent in business, as well as fervent in spirit, serving the Lord. Shew them the necessity of frugality & cleanliness, in their persons, clothes, & habitations. I wish the Methodists in Shetland, not only to be patterns of Piety, but also of frugality & cleanliness. In all the Church militant, there is not a place in rank or file for a lazy, idle, nasty Christian. When I was a missionary in the Norman Isles, my wife not only preach'd up godliness, but also cleanliness to the good women. — One who neglected both her own person, her own house & her own children, was affectionately catechised by my wife thus: "my dr Sr. G. why do you not pay more attention to your house; it is far from being clean: your children are neither clean in their clothes nor in their heads" — The good woman replied, "I hate pride: away with care for the perishing stinking body." But, (replied my wife) do you not know that Mr. Wesley has said, cleanliness is next to godliness, to which the good sister fervently replied, "Thank God, that is not in the Bible." I hope you will never meet with such dirty godliness in Shetland. I believe, God is much with you; has blessed you & will make you a blessing. Give my love to your wife — to Capt. & Mrs. ___, to the good woman (an Independant) that lives up stairs to all Mr. Robinsons, Hunries & Ads families; & tell the Twatts that Hilla is perfectly well, & does well. I & Clerm Adie send their love.
[signature]

Adam Clarkes' letter of January 2nd 1827, page three

94

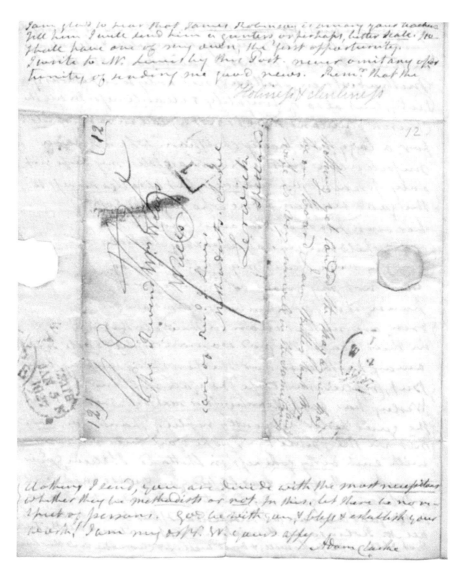

Adam Clarke's letter January 2nd 1827, page four; with the address, postal information, and some (non-transcribed) 'cross-writing'

The Reverend W. Wears,
Walls, Care of Rev. I. Lewis,
Methodist Chapel, Lerwick, Shetland
Eastcott, January 2 1827
My Dear Mr Wears,

Yours of the 21st of November. I have received this morning. But you do not mention any of my letters to you. I have written once, if not twice since I heard from you before.[151] Mr. Lowthian by my desire, has drawn among other sums, two pounds for you to repair your lodging at Bayhall and restore your ruined old boat accommodation. The Bill is come to hand and duly accepted; and all the cash £42 - in the whole, I have lodged in Mr. Smith's hands, whom I have made our Shetland Treasurer for Buildings. I also sent off October 22nd 50 Bibles, 100 Texts – 1000 picked Tracts and 200 complete catechisms, a proper proportion of which you of course, are to have. – I have sent off also about a fortnight ago, 40 new flannel petticoats, large and small, with many other articles of clothing – a whole suit & more for J. Nicholson. The best of which, I sent to Mr. Lewis –
Before that, I despatched two large Bales of Quilts, Calicoes, &c, to a great am[oun]t – & I desire that whatever the Preachers lodge there shall be left and preserved for their use, a pair of Blankets, & of calico sheets, & a quilt – that they may not be obliged to sit up all night, or lie in their clothes among straw, &c. Of the arrival of these articles, I have not yet heard. I got them in Manchester and Stockport, & they were shipped from London for Leith & Lerwick. – I wish all the

---

[150] The author would be pleased to receive from readers any suggestions of possible amendments or additions that may improve the accuracy of this transcription of Dr Adam Clarke's letter of January 2nd 1827.
[151] Mr Wears appears to eventually reply to the letters sent to him by Adam Clarke on Jan. 18, 1827; and an extract of William Wears letter was published in April 1827 in the *Wesleyan Methodist Magazine* (Vol. 50, pages 260-1), stating 'Your letters always stimulate and encourage me to persevere in the work of the Lord…I have just received a note from Mr. Lewis, with 120 of the Tracts you sent…'

Preachers and their wives to be as comfortable as possible, & I am sure I have laboured incessantly, to afford them all the help in my power.

You delight me with the account of your schools – The process[?] must reside[?] largely with you, the books which I have mentioned above. Lerwick is not the most necessitous place – where the greatest want is, there let the greatest grace abound. I wish to know whether any of our good women have lost husbands, in the deaths, in the late Greenland fishery. If there be, let me know them, their necessity, & their children. The help that I got, & sent to the 5 widows & 22 children, I hope has been long since received and applied.

The old woman left a noble testimony – I will send this to the present month's magazine. Work day[?] & night[?] while you have the light – preach Jesus and the blood of his cross – the necessity of the broken and contrite heart – salvation by faith – the witness of the Spirit and redemption from all sin. Tell the people that while evil tempers remain, they cannot be cleansed from all unrighteousness. Teach them to be diligent in business, as well as fervent in Spirit, serving the Lord. Show them the necessity of frugality and cleanliness in their persons, clothes and habitations. I wish the Methodists in Shetland, not only to be patterns of Piety, but also of frugality and cleanliness. In all the Church militant, there is not a place in rank or file for a lazy, idle, nasty Christian. When I was a missionary in the Norman Isles, my wife not only preached[?] up godliness, but also cleanliness to the good women – one who neglected both her own person, her own house & her own children, was affectionately catechized by my own wife thus: "My dear[?] L. G.[?] why do you not pay more attention to your house, it is far from being clean: your children are neither clean in their clothes nor in their heads. " The good woman replied, "I hate pride: away with care for the perishing stinking body." But (replied my wife), do you know that Mr. Wesley has said, cleanliness is next to godliness, to which the good sister fervently replied, "Thank God, that is not in the Bible!" I hope you will never meet with such dirty godliness in Shetland. I believe God is much with you; has blessed you & will make you a blessing. Give my love to your wife – to Captain and Mrs Govy, to the poor woman (an Independent) that lives upstairs – to all Mr. Robinsons, Hennies[?] & Adies[?] families: and tell the Twatts that Hilla[?] is perfectly well, and does well. J.[?] &

Clem[?] Adie send their love. I am glad to hear that James Robinson is among your teachers. Tell him I will send him a …………..[?] or perhaps, better ………[?]. I [?] shall have one of my own, the first opportunity. I write to Mr. Lewis by this post. Never omit any opportunity of sending me good news. Remember that the clothing I send, you are [to?] divide with the most necessitous, whether they be Methodists or not. In this, let there be no respect of persons. God be with you, and bless and establish your work. I am my dear Mr. W, yours affectionately, Adam Clarke.

Selected Bibliography

Adam Clarke, *A Bibliographical Dictionary* and *The Bibliographical Miscellany*, W. Baynes, Paternoster Row, London, 1802-1806.

A Letter To a Preacher on his entrance into The Work of The Ministry; also, *A Treatise On The Nature And Design Of Holy Eucharist*, London, William Tegg, 1896.

The Life of the Rev. Adam Clarke, LL.D. Compiled From Authentic Documents, By A Wesleyan Preacher, London, Joseph Smith, 193, High Holborn, 1837.

A Concise View of the Succession of Sacred Literature in a Chronological Arrangement of Authors And Their Works, from the Invention of Alphabetical Characters to the Year of our Lord 345.

Sanctification, Publishing House of the Pentecostal Church of the Nazarene, Kansas City, Missouri, n.d.

Memoirs of the Wesley Family: Collected Principally from Original Documents, London, J. Kershaw, 1823.

Commentary and Critical Notes, William Tegg and Company, 85 Queen Street, 1844, 6 Volumes.

Discourses on Various Subjects relative to the Being and Attributes of God; and His Works, in Creation, Providence, Grace, London, William Tegg, 1868, 4 Volumes.

C. H. Crookshank, *History of Methodism in Ireland*, Belfast, R. S. Allen, Son & Allen, University House, 1885, 3 Volumes.

Samuel Dunn, *Christian Theology, With A Life Of The Author*, London, William Tegg, and Co., Cheapside, 1868.

Maldwyn Edwards, *Adam Clarke*, London, Epworth Press, 1942, p.46.

J. W. Etheridge, *The Life of the Rev. Adam Clarke, LL.D.*, London, John Mason, 1858.

James Everett, *Adam Clarke Portrayed*, London, Hamilton, Adams, and Co., 1843-1849, 3 Volumes.

Robert Gallagher, *Adam Clarke: Saint and Scholar*, Belfast, Wesley Historical Society, Irish Branch, 1963.

Kenneth Geiger, *Insights into Holiness: Nineteen leading Wesleyan scholars of the Wesleyan persuasion*, Kansas City, Missouri, Beacon Hill Press, 1962.

Kenneth Geiger, *Further Insights into Holiness: Nineteen leading Wesleyan scholars present various phases of holiness thinking,* Kansas City, Missouri, Beacon Hill Press, 1963.

Kenneth Geiger, *The Word and the Doctrine: Studies in contemporary Wesleyan-Arminian theology,* Kansas City, Missouri: Beacon Hill Press, 1965.

John M. Hare, *The Life and Labours of Adam Clarke, LL.D., to which is added An Historical Sketch of the Controversy Concerning the Sonship, particularly as connected with the proceedings of the Wesleyan Methodist Conference,* London, John Stevens, 1834.

John M. Hare, *The Life and Labours of Adam Clarke, LL.D.,* London, Brown, Green, and Longmans, 1842.

John L. Peters, *Christian Perfection and American Methodism,* Nashville, Abingdon Press, 1965, p.107.

Mary Ann Smith, *An Account of the Infancy, Religious and Literary Life of Adam Clarke: written by one who was intimately acquainted with him from his boycott to the sixtieth year of his age.* ed. J.B.B. Clarke, London, T. S. Clarke, 1833, 3 Volumes.

David S. Schaff, *The Greek and Latin Creed,* Volume 11, Baker Book House, Grand Rapids, Michigan, Reprinted 1990.

Wesley Tracey, *When Adam Preached People Listened*, Beacon Hill Press of Kansas City, Missouri, 1981.

Richard Treffry, *An Enquiry into the Doctrine of the Eternal Sonship of our Lord Jesus Christ,* London, Wesleyan Conference Office, 1865.

Richard Watson, 'Remarks on the Eternal Sonship of Christ' in *The Works of The Rev. Richard Watson*, London, John Mason, 1834-1837, 12 Volumes.

John Wesley, *Letters*, John Wesley, London, Epworth Press, 1931, 8 Volumes.

John Wesley, *Works*, Bicentennial Edition, Oxford University Press, 1975-1983 and Nashville, Abingdon Press, 1984-.

John and Charles Wesley*, The Poetical Works of John and Charles Wesley,* Collected and Arranged by G. Osborn, Volume 4, p.279, London, Wesleyan-Methodist Conference Office, 1869.

Wesleyan-Methodist Magazine, 1832, p.692.

John Wesley, *Explanatory Notes upon The New Testament*, Acts 1:25, London, Wesleyan Methodist Book Room, n.d.

Books by Revd Dr Herbert Boyd McGonigle

William Cooke on Entire Sanctification, Beacon Hill Press, Kansas City, Missouri, 1978.

The Arminianism of John Wesley, Moorleys Print & Publishing, Ilkeston, Derbyshire, 1988.

John Wesley and the Moravians, Moorleys Print & Publishing, Ilkeston, Derbyshire, 1995.

John Wesley's Doctrine of Prevenient Grace, Moorleys Print & Publishing, Ilkeston, Derbyshire, 1995.

Scriptural Holiness: The Wesleyan Distinctive, Moorleys Print & Publishing, Ilkeston, Derbyshire, 1995.

Sufficient Saving Grace: John Wesley's Evangelical Arminianism, 350 pages, Paternoster Publishing, Carlisle, Cumbria, 2001.

To God Be The Glory: The Killadeas Convention 1952-2002, Moorleys Print & Publishing, Ilkeston, Derbyshire, 2002.

John Wesley's Arminian Theology: An Introduction, Moorleys Print & Publishing, Ilkeston, Derbyshire, 2005.

A Burning and a Shining Light: The Life and Ministry of William Bramwell, Moorleys Print & Publishing, Ilkeston, Derbyshire, 2009.

Christianity or Deism? John Wesley's Response to John Taylor's Denial of the Doctrine of Original Sin, Moorleys Print & Publishing, Ilkeston, Derbyshire, 2012.

John Wesley: Exemplar of the Catholic Spirit, Moorleys Print & Publishing, Ilkeston, Derbyshire, 2014.

Charles Wesley: For All, For All My Saviour Died, Moorleys Print & Publishing, Ilkeston, Derbyshire, 2014.

John Wesley: The Death of Christ, Moorleys Print & Publishing, Ilkeston, Derbyshire, 2014.

Epworth: The Cradle of Methodism, Moorleys Print & Publishing, Ilkeston, Derbyshire, 2014.

John Wesley: Doctrine of Final Judgement, Moorleys Print & Publishing, Ilkeston, Derbyshire, 2015.

Thomas Walsh: Saint and Scholar, Moorleys Print & Publishing, Ilkeston, Derbyshire, 2015.

Our Story: Autobiographical thoughts from the pen of Revd. Dr. Herbert B. McGonigle, Nazarene Theological College Archives, Manchester, 2015.